D1135301

Britain's Best Loved
CARS
All-time favourites from every decade

Britain's Best Loved CARS

All-time favourites from every decade

Matthew Leonard

Bath • New York • Singapore • Hong Kong • Cologne • Delhi
Melbourne • Amsterdam • Johannesburg • Auckland • Shenzhen

First published by Parragon in 2012
Parragon
Queen Street House
4 Queen Street
Bath BA1 1HE, UK
www.parragon.com

Design five-twentyfive.com
Consultant Richard Dredge

ISBN 978-1-4454-8809-7
Printed in China

• What's • inside...

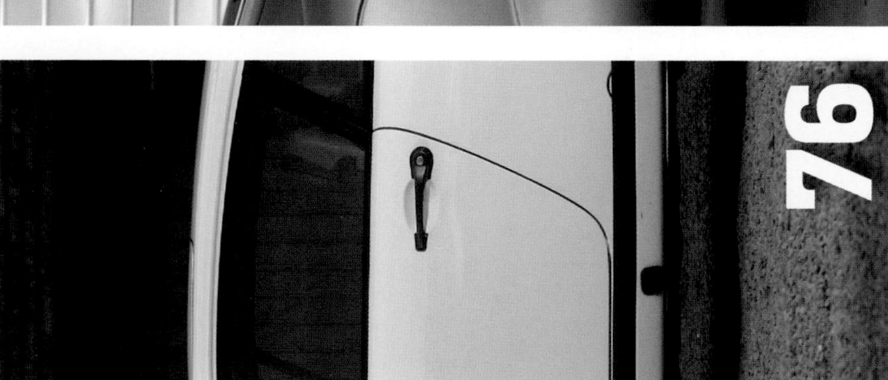

313 AMJ

Introduction

The moment that the Model T rolled off the production line, in 1908, the world was forever changed. Within just a few decades the car had become an essential part of modern life, something that people simply couldn't do without. The technological strides that the evolution of the car brought are almost impossible to define, but one thing is for certain; cars have changed society as much as society has changed cars.

Of course, once the car achieved mass popularity, then people's lives were made much easier. Everyday things such as going shopping or getting to work became so much quicker than before and our lives were simplified as a result. But, with the car came an increase in the number of roads, which in turn lead to the creation of motorways, which lead to cars getting quicker, which lead to more accidents. The reliance of the car on oil helped to create vast inequality in standards of wealth, not to mention wars and dubious approaches to foreign policy by Western governments, in particular. Added to these problems are concerns over the damage that so many cars may be causing to the environment, which along with the increasing dependence on oil, has influenced the prevailing thoughts and ideas on the cars of the future, some of which are starting to appear on the streets today.

This book traces the evolution of the car in Britain since the 1960s and examines how and why the cars we drive, or dream of driving, have come into being. With the use

Cars have changed society as much as society has changed cars

of comprehensive lists of top 10 bestsellers compiled from a multitude of sources, a slightly more arbitrary choice of cars within the various classes and fantastic period photographs, discover how the British public's taste in cars has been shaped over the years.

In just over 50 years cars have gone from functional vehicles, such as the Vauxhall Viva, to incredible performance machines, like the Bugatti Veyron. They have become far more than just tools, cars are now inextricably linked to our lives and their design and form embodies and mirrors who and what we are, and more importantly what we believe in.

The 1908 Model T crank.

UFX 3

1960s

10 Bestsellers

For the motor industry the 1960s was a decade of innovation and evolution when cars took a leap forward, in terms of design and ability, from the vehicles of the post-war period. This paradigm shift was not so much led by technical innovations in the car industry, but rather a change in the country's ageing road network; the days of driving long distances on slow, single-lane roads were numbered. The motorways were coming and when the first part of the M1 was finished, in November 1959, it heralded a new way to travel. These big high-speed super-highways would open up a whole new world of travel and opportunity to a generation that still had memories of the horse and cart.

Motorways are something that we take for granted these days. They are so much part of the fabric of the landscape that we barely notice them. But back in 1960 they were the gateway to adventure and travel. As their building continued apace, car manufacturers began their own revolution in design. Cars would become more powerful, faster and durable, but most importantly of all, they were to become more accessible to the average person. Along with sporty models like the MGB GT, the 1960s gave birth to great family cars like the BMC 1100/1300, Ford Cortina and Mini. These vehicles sold in huge numbers as buyers realised that the barriers to a new world had been thrown open, and the key to a shiny new car was all that was required to drive through them.

of the 1960s

1.

• STATS AND FACTS •

FAWLTY MOTORS

The Austin 1100 Countryman was famously given a 'damn good thrashing' by Basil Fawlty in the Gourmet Nights episode of the timeless sit-com, *Fawlty Towers*.

DESIGN LEGEND

Sir Alec Issigonis was the designer of the BMC 1100/1300. He also designed the classic Mini, for which he is more fondly remembered.

The MG 1300 cut a dash with its two-tone colour scheme; it was the sporty option for ADO16 buyers.

BMC 1100/1300

The BMC 1100/1300 range stems from a time when British manufacturing power dominated the car market in Britain. Although there were foreign manufacturers producing quality products, British people bought British products and the BMC 1100 and 1300 were by far the bestselling cars of the 1960s, fending off competition from Ford's Cortina, Vauxhall's Viva and Austin's own Mini.

The design was based on the BMC AD016 blueprint, which gave birth to a plethora of cars manufactured by the members of the British Motor Corporation (BMC). All these cars were essentially the same model, with differing specifications. They were an early example of badge engineering, which is still commonplace in car production today. Examples of badge-engineered AD016s were Austin, Morris, MG, Wolseley or Vanden Plas versions of the 1100 and 1300, plus the Riley Kestrel. The Austin and Morris editions sold the most in Britain during the 1960s, hence their place at the top of the list.

Built by the British Motor Corporation, the Morris 1100 was launched in 1962 amidst much fanfare and excitement, with the Austin version launched soon after. A new Morris 1100 could be bought for the princely sum of £675, with the deluxe version an extra £20, boasting such extras as front door pockets and a passenger sun visor. The MkI was renowned for its innovative hydrolastic suspension, front-wheel drive and spacious cabin, bringing an affordable family car to the burgeoning market.

'When you're designing a new car for production, never, never copy the opposition'
Sir Alec Issigonis

In 1967, BMC released a MkII version, fitted with a 1275cc engine and known as the 1300. The MkII was a great success and long waiting lists soon accrued, both at home and abroad. The MkII was distinguished from its predecessor by a slightly wider front grille and smoother tail lights, but otherwise it looked very similar.

The Austin 1100 followed hot on the heels of its Morris sibling.

2. Ford Cortina

Ford's Cortina first appeared on the streets of Britain at the beginning of the decade and it never looked back. Coming a close second to the AD016 during the 1960s, by the end of the 1970s it was the king of the road. The MkI Cortina was a compact and affordable car that spawned four further generations. The success of the model is highlighted by the fact that every Mark sold over one million units, making it one of the most successful cars ever to grace the road.

The MkI was launched in September 1962 and, bizarrely, it was the success of a small car that gave birth to the larger Cortina. Ford felt that it could not compete with BMC's Mini, so it set about building a car that would dominate the other end of the market. Initially available with either a 1.2 or 1.5-litre engine, the Ford Consul Cortina, as it was called until the MkI's first upgrade in 1964, was a rear-wheel drive vehicle that offered a great deal for the price tag.

• STATS AND FACTS •

CARRY ON CORTINA

Hattie Jacques' 'Glam Cabs', in the film *Carry on Cabby*, famously used the Ford Cortina, while Sid James' competing company used outdated Austin taxis.

DECADES OF SUCCESS

The Ford Cortina was so succesful that it remained in production for 20 years. No fewer than five generations were offered in that time.

In 1966 the MkII version was released and it sported a more conservative styling and modern look. It came with a new 1.3-litre engine and the 1.5-litre was replaced by a 1.6-litre unit. By 1967 the Cortina was the most popular car in Britain, setting it up for a stunning future as the country's car of choice.

The Cortina MkI came with a multitude of engine, trim and bodystyle options.

The Viva HA was a turning point for Vauxhall.

3. Vauxhall Viva (HA and HB)

The Viva was Vauxhall's first small car since 1936 and a direct competitor to the Ford 100E and Morris Minor. Produced in two versions between 1963 and 1970, the basic saloon cost £436, with the De-Luxe model an extra £32. The HA version had a 44bhp 1057cc engine which would prove to be very popular, with some 100,000 built within the first ten months. The HB version was even more successful, with 556,752 produced between late 1966 and October 1970. The HB had distinctive Coke bottle styling that was to become such a feature of cars of the era and proved to be a worthy successor to the HA.

The HA version of the Viva was only available as a two-door saloon, but there was a van version too. This proved to be very popular, especially with the General Post Office (GPO), which bought thousands of them and painted them yellow, creating a ubiquitous presence along the roads of Britain. Amazingly, due to its very large corporate presence, the van stayed in production right through until 1983, which was years past its sell-by date.

• STATS AND FACTS •

SPOILT FOR CHOICE

The Viva was initially only available in two versions – Base and De-Luxe. In 1965 a Super-Deluxe version was added.

BUILD QUALITY

Corrosion problems were so bad on the early Vivas that often large parts of the car simply fell off, earning them a terrible reputation for rotting.

4. Mini

The Mini was born in 1959, as the Austin Seven and Morris Mini-Minor. For its makers, BMC, the Mini was not a car that delivered much profit. Indeed, this was one of the main reasons why Ford decided to proceed with the Cortina. However, BMC was able to turn a small profit from each car produced due to the mark up on the Cooper and Cooper S models. The Mini is most famous for its starring role in *The Italian Job*, starring Michael Caine.

• STATS AND FACTS •

ESSENCE OF THE 1960S
The Mini was a 1960's icon and along with rock n roll and the mini-skirt, it defined the decade.

RECORD BREAKER
Over 5.3 million of the original Minis were sold, making it the best-selling British car ever made.

5. Rootes Arrow range

Rootes' status in the bestseller list of the 1960s comes thanks to the company's philosophy of producing the same car under a range of badges. Even so, the Arrow range only just outsold Vauxhall's Victor. Of all the versions that Rootes produced, the Hillman Hunter was the most successful. The final Hunter to be built, this time by Chrysler, was in 1979, but a version of the car was still being made in Iran as late as 2005!

• STATS AND FACTS •

TARGET RANGE
The Rootes Arrow range was produced between 1966 and 1979. The range included models by Chrysler, Hillman, Sunbeam and Singer.

CATERING FOR ALL TASTES
The Arrow range covered all the main body styles such as the saloon and estate, but the coupé models were only produced by Sunbeam.

6. Vauxhall Victor

Vauxhall began production of the Victor in 1957 and by the mid-1960s it was a popular choice in Britain. The Victor FB, unveiled in 1961, had a top speed of 76mph and could manage 0-60 in 23 seconds. A sporty version, the VX4/90, featured a twin-carburettor engine producing an impressive 71bhp. The FC series followed in 1964, followed by the FD in 1967. The FD version gave rise to the powerful Ventora, which married the Victor's frame to a 3.3-litre engine.

• STATS AND FACTS •

GLOBAL IMPACT
By 1961, the success of the Vauxhall Victor at home was being emulated abroad and the Victor had become Britain's most exported car.

101 CHANGES
The FC Victor was marketed as the Victor 101, a reference to the fact that there were '101 improvements' over the FB.

Buyers of the early Mini could choose Austin or Morris versions, each with an 848cc engine.

The Rootes Arrow range featured crisp, modern styling, with a multitude of versions on offer.

The 101 was part of the launch line up of the third-generation Victor, otherwise known as the FC.

The Anglia 105E stood out, with its reverse-rake rear window.

7. Ford Anglia

By the start of the 1960s, the Ford Anglia, in one version or another, had been available since before World War II. The release of the Anglia 105E, in 1959, was to be the car's final incarnation, with production ceasing in 1967. The car was very American in style with its sweeping lines and prominent fins but, from 1961 onwards, a more conventional-looking estate version was also available. The Anglia will be remembered for its unrivalled reliability and hardiness; it was only the success of the Cortina that overshadowed it. A sporty Anglia, the Super Anglia 123E, was also available from 1962.

• STATS AND FACTS •

MAGICAL MOMENTS
The Ford Anglia is most recognisable in the movie world as the flying car in the Harry Potter films.

GROUND BREAKER
The Anglia was one of the first cars to have metallic paint. Two colours, Venetian Gold and Blue Mink, were offered.

The Escort replaced the 105E, and was far more modern.

8. Ford Escort

The Escort was only released in 1968, but it had such an impact on British motorists that by the beginning of 1970 it had sold more than 177,000 units. The car was to be a huge success for Ford and it was the model that cemented the company as a household name in Britain. It debuted at the Brussels Motor Show in 1968 and was designed to be the replacement for the now ancient Anglia. The MkI was the first of six generations of Escort that would come over the next four decades. It was a remarkable car that showed just how good Ford was, with a version available for everyone, whatever they wanted from a car.

• STATS AND FACTS •

FIRST OF A KIND
The awesome Escort MK1 RS2000 was the forerunner to the modern hot hatch, laying the groundwork for models such as the XR3i.

A-FORD-ABLE CARS
In 1969 the cheapest Ford Escort available was the saloon, priced at £672. The most expensive was the 1300GT, which cost £851.

The Corsair was always overshadowed by the Cortina.

9. Ford Corsair

Like the Cortina, the Corsair name was originally prefixed with the word Consul. It came to market in 1963 and production continued until 1970, although after 1965 the Consul name was dropped. The Corsair was available as either a four-door saloon or estate, with a two-door edition available to special order. Larger than the Cortina, the Corsair was powered by the same 1.5-litre Kent engine, but it was never anything like as popular as the Cortina. Indeed the MkIII Cortina was the replacement for the Corsair. Only 310,000 were ever built, but it paved the way for better cars.

• STATS AND FACTS •

V4 VERY NEARLY
The original slogan for the Corsair was 'The car that is seen but not heard', but soon changed to 'I've got a V in my bonnet', a nod to the car's V4 engine.

AMERICAN HERITAGE
The Corsair's sloped bonnet design was a direct homage to the classic Ford Thunderbird, which was popular in the United States.

Great fun to drive, but early Imps were very unreliable.

10. Hillman Imp

Hillman was part of the Rootes Group, which manufactured the Imp from 1963 until 1976. The car was rear-engined and over the course of its life there were three body styles offered; saloon, coupé and estate. Like all the Rootes cars, badge-engineered versions were also released, such as the Singer Chamois, launched in 1964 and the Sunbeam Sport, which arrived in 1966. The Imp was plagued with production problems and the car's reputation suffered greatly as a result. A revised and improved version was released in 1966, but the Imp never really recovered from the image it had already acquired.

• STATS AND FACTS •

A HIGHLAND FLING
The Imp was often the first car that many Scots owned and is so famous that it was chosen to appear on a tapestry depicting the history of Scotland.

A STRONG START
Approximately 500,000 Imps were produced, 50 per cent of which came in the first three years of its life.

Minis and Saloons

As the 1960s began, car manufacturers turned their attention towards the mass market. However, the infancy of the industry during the early part of the 1960s meant that most cars on the road were of the mini and saloon variety, but this lack of choice would not last long.

BMC's 1100 and Ford's Cortina dominated the top ten best-selling cars of the 1960s, thanks to their affordability and the range of engines and trims on offer. But these weren't the only cars available; there were several other makes and models which helped to drive the British motor industry forward.

Due to the sheer number of companies within the group, not to mention its market share, BMC produced several cars tailored to people who did not suit its more popular models. One of these was the **Morris Oxford**, a saloon (and occasionally an estate too) that became a common sight in the British suburbs. Oxford was a brand that Morris had used before, as the original version was introduced in 1919; indeed it was the first car ever produced by William Morris. It was named Oxford after Morris' hometown. By 1960 the Oxford was on its fifth generation and in 1961 the Oxford MkVI was released. It was part of BMC's Farina range (so called because the cars were designed by Pininfarina), which included other models such as the **Wolseley 15/60** and the **MG Magnette MkIII**. The Oxford MkVI was produced by BMC for a decade and the diesel-engined version of the car was a popular choice as a taxi, further exposing the car to the public and doubtless prolonging its life. All in all, just short of 210,000 Oxford MkVIs were produced.

The Farina range looked just like Peugeot's 404, which was also designed by Italian design house Pininfarina.

Another popular saloon of the decade was the **Austin Cambridge**. In 1961 the A55 Austin Cambridge was updated to become

the **A60 Cambridge**. It was the latest in a long list of Cambridges that had started in the early 1950s and it would become a popular alternative to the Cortina and 1100. Like the Oxford, the Cambridge was produced by BMC and was from its Farina range. Also like the Oxford, the car was a popular choice for cabbies, not just in Britain but in Hong Kong. Indeed it's estimated that the 1967 taxi versions of the Cambridge accounted for some 18 per cent of sales and that almost 30 per cent of the taxis in Hong Kong were made by BMC.

The A60 had a top speed of just over 80mph and could reach 60mph in a little under 20 seconds, which was not bad at all. When production of the Cambridge came to an end almost 280,000 had been produced and this, along with the 210,000 Oxfords, accounted for a respectable portion of the saloon car market.

The Austin A60 Cambridge was slightly longer in wheelbase and wider in track than the A55.

Another saloon car of note from the 1960s is the **Rover P6**. Available from 1963, the P6 was an advanced car for its time, featuring such developments as disc brakes for every wheel, a fully synchronised transmission and a de Dion rear suspension system. The car was produced in several series and overall some 320,000 were built over its 14-year lifespan. But the real claim to fame for Rover's car was that it won the first ever European Car of the Year award, in 1964. This did wonders for its sales figures and helped to further the development of car technology. The car industry, particularly in Britain, was woefully uncompetitive and these high-profile awards forced rival car makers to up their game, which ultimately benefitted the consumer.

The Rover P6 was the first ever winner of the European Car of the Year award

These larger saloon cars filled a gap in the market and catered for those that were not interested in the mass market products from Ford and BMC. The cars were larger than the average car, fairly powerful for their day and their size enabled them to hold the road well and deliver a smooth drive. They gave their owners a feeling of individuality, and to some degree luxury, and alerted the car companies to the possibilities of expanding ranges and increasing profits through high-end models. It was a trend that would continue to grow.

In 3.5-litre V8 form, the Rover P6, or 3500, became a seriously quick family luxury express.

The Imp was superbly practical, with a hatchback plus a boot in the front, as it was rear-engined.

There was also a market for smaller vehicles that were not aimed at the family. The Mini utterly dominated this market but it was a particularly small 'small car'. Other models such as the **Volkswagen Beetle**, **Ford Anglia 100E** and the **Hillman Imp** were also popular and they were all cheap to run, nippy and, like the larger saloon cars, allowed an expression of individuality.

It is fair to say that the Beetle, Anglia and Imp were the 'best of the rest' because none of them had a chance against the Mini. The **Mini** was more than a car; it was the harbinger of a cultural revolution, an era-defining object that is still hugely sought after today. The Mini even catered for the person who required a slightly bigger small car, in the form of the **Mini Traveller**, memorable for the stick-on wood panelling along its side. In 1969 the Traveller, and its cousin the **Countryman**, were replaced by the Mini Clubman estate, but it was the original Mini that was by far the most popular model. If the production figures for the Imp and the Mini are compared it becomes clear how the Mini dwarfed the competition. By 1976, 13 years after the Imp was first available, the Rootes Group had sold 440,000 units, which is an impressive figure. But the Mini reached one million sales by 1965 – just six years after its debut. By this time the car had won the Monte Carlo Rally and the Thousand Lake Rally, in Finland, which boosted the image of the road car still further. The Mini earned its creator, Alec Issigonis, a knighthood in 1969 and by the time he died, in 1988, aged 82, more than four million Minis had been sold.

The 1960s was as much a time of change for car manufacturers operating in the UK as it was for the population. It should not be underestimated how much the country

MINIS / SALOONS OF THE 60S

1. Morris Oxford
2. Wolseley 15/60
3. MG Magnette MkIII
4. Austin A60 Cambridge
5. Rover P6
6. Mini
7. Volkswagen Beetle
8. Ford Anglia 100E
9. Hillman Imp
10. Mini Traveller/ Countryman

Estate versions of the Mini mixed style with practicality.

The Mini was more than a car; it was the harbinger of a cultural revolution

The original Beetle is the biggest-selling car of all time, with over 21 million examples built – a figure which is unlikely ever to be beaten thanks to such a long production run.

was still suffering from the effects of World War II. Only 15 years before the decade had begun the country was being told to be conservative and harbour resources. Technological development and industrial prowess had been focused on the war effort, not the improvement of people's lives. These factors were all too evident in the car market during the 1960s, where choices were restricted and invariably all rather similar. People could either have an average car or a better version of an average car. But, as people started to move on from the recent past and the industry geared up for the new, post-war world, cars like the Mini began to show how companies could attract new buyers and how consumers could stand out from the crowd. A new dawn was creeping over the horizon and within a decade things would be very different.

The Rover P6 was one of the safest cars of the era, thanks to its monocoque (single shell) construction.

ROVER 2000

SC. TC. OCH SC AUTOMATIC

Speed, power and the open road

The 1960s was an era of innovation and technological progress and the car was at the forefront of these changes, powering humanity into a new era of speed, technology and independence. These changes were epitomised by two events – the building of the M1, in England and the Le Mans 24-hour race, in France.

By the turn of the decade, the first stretch of the M1 was operational and throughout the 1960s a series of extensions were added, stretching the road from London, in the south, to Leeds, in the north, halving journey times and heralding a giant stride in the fortunes of the car manufacturing industry.

The Pace of progress

Cars became far less utilitarian, with manufacturers releasing powerful models that could take advantage of these new and faster roads. In 1959, the Jaguar MkII heralded the birth of a new type of car – the GT. The GT version of the classic MGB was released in 1962, to great acclaim. MG's advertising campaign featured the MGB GT driving along the M1, tempting customers to enjoy the new attractions that the motorway offered; speed, freedom and opportunity. The MGB GT had a top speed of 105mph, shattering the previous speed limit of earlier production cars. Until 1964 there were no speed limits on UK motorways, but the technological progression that the motorway enabled

Top: The new motorway network slashed journey times.
Centre: Race tracks were much more relaxed about safety.
Bottom: There was far more cameraderie in motorsport then.

meant that the days of unconfined speeds on British roads were short-lived. In 1965 a temporary speed limit of 70mph was installed, which was made permanent in 1967.

Le Mans

One place where there were no speed limits was at the Le Mans 24-hour race. The 1960s was the defining decade for Le Mans, with Ferrari dominating the race, usurping Maserati and Aston Martin as the pre-eminent force in motorsport. The Testarossa and GTO conquered all before them and it wasn't until the latter half of the decade that the industrial might of Ford turned the tables with the GT40, a car capable of speeds well in excess of 200mph. It is no secret that many of the developments in production cars are powered by their racing counterparts and this was graphically displayed during the 1960s at Le Mans. Manufacturers such as Alfa Romeo, Porsche and Renault came to the fore, but over 50 companies built cars that competed for the trophy, driving forward innovations that soon began to make their way to the roads of Britain and Europe. The new breed of racing cars fascinated the public and Le Mans regularly received crowds of over 300,000 spectators, crammed in to the circuit, watching from the side of the track with little or no safety measures to protect them. The sounds, smells and palpable excitement that these fantastic machines produced were to instigate even greater changes in the coming years, both on and off the track.

At home, the motorway was seen as the domestic incarnation of the racetrack. It allowed driving to become something more than simply a means of getting from A to B. From now on, cars were to become an expression of freedom, status and joy. They were objects of desire, for the first time available to the masses, and driving would never be quite the same again.

Top: Le Mans was as iconic in the 1960s as it is now.
Centre: Racing allowed car makers to build better road cars.
Bottom: The opening of the M1 marked the dawn of a new era.

Rolls-Royce has always represented the pinnacle of road car luxury. Shown here is an early Silver Shadow.

Luxury Cars

Ever since the first vehicle was produced there has been a market for luxury cars. By the 1960s this was well understood by manufacturers, but mass-market car production was still in its infancy and the 1960s provided a steep learning curve that led to the rapid development of the luxury car.

In the pre-war era cars themselves were seen as a luxury and just the idea of owning a car for personal use was a dream to many people. But, in the 1960s, society was changing and as car production exploded into life the luxury end of the market became one that carmakers began to pay more attention to. By the start of the decade most of the major car manufacturers produced a model version that was considered 'top of the range' and generally luxury cars were nicer versions of the standard model. For example, BMC made several high-end versions of their popular A60 Farina range, such as the Austin Wolseley 6/99 and 6/110, and the Austin Westminster.

These cars were still fairly subtle in design and fitted the era of bowler hats and grey suits. However, they were larger than the average saloon car and they were also generally more powerful and refined.

The **Austin Westminster** series had began life in 1954 with the A90 and by the start of the 1960s the series had evolved to the A99. The car incorporated a 2.9-litre straight 6 engine that, thanks to its twin carburettors, could generate 103bhp, which propelled the car to 98mph and allowed a respectable 0–60 time of around 15 seconds. A synchromesh 3-speed gearbox was standard as were power assisted disc brakes. The **Wolseley 6/99** and

These cars were still fairly subtle in design and fitted the era of bowler hats and grey suits

BMC's six-cylinder Farina range offered understated luxury at a relatively affordable price. This is an Austin A99 Westminster.

The Vanden Plas Princess 3-litre sat at the top of BMC's six-cylinder Farina range.

In 1964, a brand new Austin A110 Super de Luxe cost £1,112

the **Vanden Plas Princess** versions of the A99 Westminster, as well as the Westminster itself, were all fairly conservative in their appearance, although the Vanden Plas was the most luxurious of the bunch. Still, they had a certain look of authority that distinguished them from the crowd and it was clear that not everyone could afford to buy one of these luxury cars.

In 1961 the A99 was given a facelift and renamed the A110. The new version was slightly wider, which allowed for more room in the back and improved the road holding. The Vanden Plas Princess MkII also added refinements such as air conditioning, drop-down tables for the rear passengers, walnut

Another six-cylinder Farina was the Wolseley 6/110.

The Ford Zephyr and Zodiac MkIII were large family saloons for those who wanted space on a relative budget.

surrounds and better upholstery. The A110 was fitted with a more powerful engine that increased the top speed to over the 100mph mark. BMC also updated the Wolseley in 1961, which became known as the 6/110. The **6/110** was to set the standard for luxurious but affordable cars of the era. It was powerful,

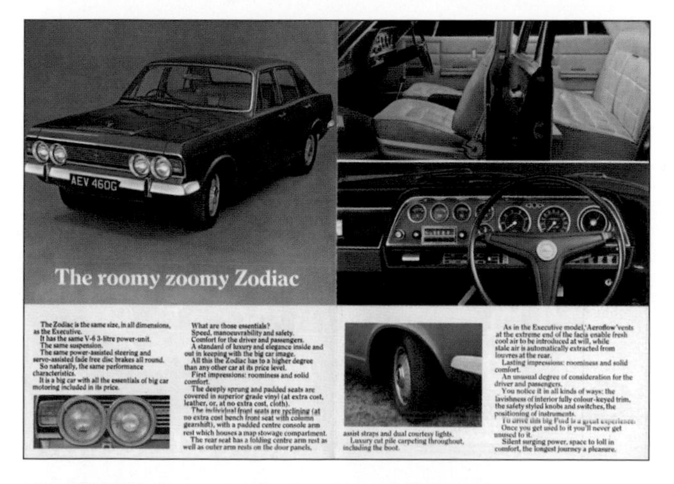

The MkIV Zephyr and Zodiac were very boxy compared with their predecessors, so they weren't as popular.

had an imposing grille, which was topped off by an illuminated badge, and inside the car was given a glorious makeover. Not to be outdone by Vanden Plas, BMC added walnut fascias and door cappings along with opulent, deep-pile carpeting.

Other car makers offered their own luxury versions of mainstream cars. Ford produced the **Zephyr MkIII**, still replete with fins and chrome, although perhaps a bit more subdued for the British market, and in 1965 it introduced an Executive option for its **Zodiac**, which upped the stakes again. Electric window washers, a cigar lighter, clock and reversing lights were all fitted as standard, as were padded leather seats. Away from these everyday models there was a select band of manufacturers producing absolute refinement that was out of reach for the majority.

Among these tailors to the elite were companies such as Daimler, Rolls-Royce and

The Daimler V8 250 used the same bodyshell as the Jaguar MKII, but instead of a straight-six up front there was a V8. Unfortunately this proved to be unreliable, as it wasn't really up to the job of powering such a huge car.

Jaguar. Daimler's two notable cars of the 1960s were the 2.5 V8 and the V8 250. The 2.5 V8 was so named because of the engine it used (a 2.5-litre V8); as Daimler buyers expected, the cabin featured lashings of wood and leather. It was based on the Jaguar MkII, as that company had acquired Daimler in 1960. Indeed, the 2.5 V8 was the first Daimler produced, after its purchase by Jaguar. With a top speed of 112mph and capable of 0–60 in just 13.5 seconds, the 2.5 V8 cost the princely sum of £1,770. The updated version of the 2.5 was the **V8 250**, which was very similar in design, but further refined the already luxurious 2.5 with the introduction of ventilated leather seats, which also reclined. In 1968 the **XJ6** replaced the 250, cementing Jaguar's place in the luxury market.

Rolls-Royce released its **Silver Shadow** in October 1965. It was the height of luxury and set the standard for the high-end cars to come. The Silver Shadow was fitted with a 6.23-litre V8 engine, which was later enlarged to 6.75 litres. The workmanship on the car was exquisite and the occupants were cocooned in a world of wood, leather and

‘Take the best that exists and make it better. When it does not exist, design it’

Sir Henry Royce

The Silver Shadow was the first monocoque-construction car to be offered by Rolls-Royce.

deep carpeting. The drive was almost silent and the rear passengers could relax with a drink from the on-board cabinet. In its first year of production a Silver Shadow would set back the discerning gentleman £6,557, a fine price for such luxury.

LUXURY CARS OF THE 60S

1. Wolseley 6/99
2. Austin Westminster
3. Vanden Plas Princess
4. Wolseley 6/110
5. Ford Zephyr MkIII
6. Ford Zodiac
7. Daimler V8 250
8. Jaguar XJ6
9. Rolls-Royce Silver Shadow

The Silver Shadow and Daimler’s 2.5-litre road-palaces were the very height of 1960s road-going luxury and they distinguished their occupants from the masses around them. But, such a scenario was nothing new. Rolls-Royce had been making cars since 1904, while Daimler had built its first car almost a decade before, in 1896. The difference during the 1960s was that the car, in general, was becoming more affordable, and hence more attainable, for the common man. In the early part of the twentieth century, despite Henry Ford’s protestations to the contrary, most people had little or no chance of affording a car, but now the dream was more attainable. As a result, it would not be long before the average person would want the luxury that was more associated with the rich and famous. Soon, all car manufacturers would start to offer upmarket versions of their standard cars, charging that little bit extra for a taste of the high life.

The luxury car market was developing and would only get bigger. From now on the good life, or at least a taste of it, was available to all, and the car industry would take full advantage.

Arguably the most sensuous road car ever made: the Jaguar E-Type, here in Series 1 roadster form.

Sports Cars

Whether it was Jaguar's E-Type at Le Mans or Issigonis' Mini in Monte Carlo, the 1960s brought the thrill of speed to the public. As fast cars became available to the masses and the road network expanded at home, sports cars would become permanent fixtures on the streets of Britain.

By the start of the 1960s the car had started to become much more that just a means of transport. As designs improved and form started to catch up with function there was a massive increase in the number of fast cars produced and sold. The 1960s saw the birth of the production sports car, which has since been a constant fixture on our roads. The decade produced some of the finest speed machines ever made, and several of the models that were introduced during the 1960s are still manufactured today, albeit in their newer

guises. These models, such as the Porsche 911, shared the roads of Britain with timeless classics like Jaguar's E-Type, making the 1960s a heyday for the sports car.

During the decade, Le Mans played a vital role in the development of the car. It was from this gruelling race that one of the finest sports cars ever made was born – the **Jaguar 3.8-litre E-Type**. The E-Type was the logical progression of Jaguar's D-Type, which had performed so well at Le Mans during the 1950s. The D-Type came to prominence at the circuit in 1954, when it finished as runner up, and then again in controversial circumstances in 1955, the year in which the worst ever motorsport accident took place. In this, Pierre Levegh's Mercedes was clipped on the final bend and careered into the crowd, killing more than 80 people, but nevertheless the race continued and was won by Mike Hawthorn and Ivor Bueb in their Jaguar D-Type.

One of the most valuable cars ever made: the Ferrari 250 GTO. Just 39 were built.

It may have been a rather dubious victory, but the D-Type went from strength to strength, winning the 1956 Le Mans, beating Aston Martin and Ferrari, and taking five of the top six places at Le Mans in 1957. By the start of the 1960s the D-Type was obsolete, but it had set the foundations for the E-Type. In 1961 the car was revealed to great acclaim at the Geneva Motor Show and it continued to be produced, in one version or another, for the next 14 years, selling more than 70,000 units. The car was built in two-seater roadster and coupé, plus 2+2 coupé bodystyles, and sold all around the world, doing particularly well in the United States, where some 80 per cent of the models produced were sold.

The E-Type's success not only stemmed from its racing heritage; it was relatively affordable, with its £2,000 price tag at launch. Plus it was also reliable, beautifully styled and fast with a 150mph top speed. With disc brakes all round and independent rear suspension, it handled and stopped brilliantly too. After 1966 the car was fitted with a 4.2 litre engine, increasing the available power and performance and ensuring that it remained one of the most desirable cars in the world.

Perhaps the most curvaceous car ever created – the AC Cobra, seen here in 427 (7-litre) form.

SPORTS CARS OF THE 60S

1. Jaguar E-Type
2. AC Cobra
3. Triumph TR6
4. Aston Martin DB4
5. Ferrari 250 GTO
6. Mini Cooper S
7. Porsche 911

The E-Type was by no means alone in the UK sports car market during the 1960s. Other cars such as the **AC Cobra**, **Triumph TR6**, **Aston Martin DB4** and, of course, the legendary **Ferrari 250 GTO**, all emerged as competitors to Jaguar's masterpiece. But there was another, smaller car, that vied for the attention of fast car enthusiasts, and one that was to be a huge success over the years to come; the **Mini Cooper S**.

Alec Issigonis' Mini became an iconic car on Britain's roads and epitomised the 1960s. The Cooper S was the racing version of this little classic and it achieved great success in the Monte Carlo rallies. The S version was the brainchild of John Cooper, owner of the eponymous Formula 1 world champion team of 1959 and 1960. In 1964 a 1275cc version was released that proved to be one of the definitive

Enzo Ferrari described the Jaguar E-type as 'the most beautiful car ever made'

Minis racing at Silverstone in 1965.

sports cars of its generation. In 1964 it won the Monte Carlo rally, propelling the little racer into the upper echelons of motorsport. The Cooper S won the Monte Carlo again in 1965, and in 1966 it finished first, second and third, sweeping the board, and although the results were later overturned on a technicality, it won again in 1967. During the 1960s, rallying was a big draw in motor racing and it allowed a British-made car the opportunity for world renown. Although now made by BMW, the Mini Cooper S is still one of the popular cars on the road.

Our last model to explore in the world of 1960s sports cars is the breathtaking **Porsche 911**. To this day it remains one of the most sought after sports cars in the world, but its roots lie in the 1960s. Introduced for the first time at the Frankfurt Motor Show, in 1963, the 911 was continually improved upon, leading to an S version in 1967, producing some 160bhp. But perhaps it is the iconic Targa version that secured its place in motoring history, even though Triumph had offered a broadly similar roof concept with its TR4 several years earlier; it coined the term Surrey Top however, instead of Targa. Many have tried to copy the Porsche ethos over the years, but few have succeeded. It was so groundbreaking and popular that to many people the Porsche 911 was, and still is, the ultimate sports car in the world.

Still on sale since it debuted in 1963, the 911 has always featured a rear-mounted flat-six engine.

1970s

10 Bestsellers

After the heyday of the 1960s, the 1970s saw a downturn in the fortunes of the British car industry. Outdated working practices, strikes and social unrest all contributed to the beginning of the end for the great British car.

In the twilight years of the 1960s, the status of BMC as the best-selling manufacturer in the UK was under serious threat from Ford. This intrusion in the market continued as the American giant was joined by other foreign makes, such as Peugeot, which began to squeeze the UK companies out of the arena. British manufacturers had long seen this coming and several attempts were made to arrest the decline, but to little avail. In 1966, BMC and Jaguar merged to create British Motor Holdings (BMH) but this couldn't stop the slide and in 1968 Leyland, which also owned Triumph and Rover, joined with BMH, creating the British Leyland Motor Corporation (BLMC) in a desperate attempt to prevent the seemingly inevitable.

Despite everything, by the end of the decade the BLMC had appealed to the government for financial help, resulting in its nationalisation as British Leyland. It was too little too late and by the start of the 1980s British Leyland stood alone as the last bastion of the British motor industry, lost in a world that had passed it by. This was bad news for UK industry, but good news for the consumer. Car buyers would now have more choice, better products and ultimately, a better ownership experience.

of the 1970s

1.

STATS AND FACTS

TV COMEBACK

The 2006 television series, *Life on Mars*, made the Cortina cool again. Perhaps even cooler than it was before, as the Coke-bottle styling wasn't to everyone's taste at the time.

STRONG PEDIGREE

The Cortina was produced in five generations, making it a common sight in the towns and cities of Britain. The last generation was called the Cortina 80.

The Cortina MkIII featured distinctive Coke-bottle styling. This is a range-topping GXL model.

Ford Cortina

When it comes to the number one car of the 1970s there is one clear favourite – the Ford Cortina. During the decade two Cortina models together accounted for by far the highest amount of new car sales. The first to be released, in 1970, was the MkIII, which continued to be produced until 1976. Up until the MkIII Cortina's release, standard production cars had tended to be very conservative in design, but the MkIII looked more American than European. The new Cortina showed off sweeping lines that curved along the length of the car. As a result, the car looked ahead of its time and wasn't to everyone's taste, but those who disliked Ford's new car were in the minority.

The MkIII was released in several different versions, with engine sizes ranging from the basic 1300cc, through to the popular 1600cc, and also a larger capacity 2-litre model, both of which featured an overhead camshaft design. The GT and GXL models represented the top of the range and featured such refinements as sports wheels, halogen lights and multi-dialled dashboards. The success of the MkIII led to Ford further developing the Cortina, and in 1976 the MkIV was released.

The MkIV saw a return to the traditional boxy style of the 1960s and 70s and it had more in common, at least externally, with the MkI and II Cortinas. The MkIV saw the introduction of the 'Ghia' badge, indicating the range-topping model, and the brand was to remain a Ford staple for years to come. Ghia was originally an Italian design house but Ford bought it and reduced it to a mere trim level, sadly. Ford also introduced a 2.3-litre V6 version of the MkIII but it was seen as too expensive to run and insure. In the late 1970s the MkIV Cortina was the most popular new car in Britain, but there are probably fewer than 250 of them remaining today.

The Cortina family came in all shapes and colours.

2. Ford Escort

The MkI Ford Escort was released in 1968, but remained in production until 1974 and replaced the ageing Anglia. The car was a runaway success and in mid-1974 Ford achieved the two-millionth sale, making it Ford's most successful car to date, but also helping the British economy as approximately 60 per cent of the cars had been built in Britain.

Not only was the car a big success on the roads, but it also took the rally world by storm. In 1970, the MkI won the London to Mexico World Cup Rally, which gave rise to the legendary Escort Mexico road car, a direct nod to the rally victory.

In 1975 the MkII was released in L, GL, Sport, RS Mexico and Ghia versions. It continued to sell well and also kept up with the pace in the rally world, as the MkII won the RAC Rally every year between 1975 and 1979. These early Escorts marked the beginning of a long-running career for the car and between its inception and the end of its production life, in 1998, it sold more than four million units.

• STATS AND FACTS •

CREAM OF THE CROP
In the 1970s Ford's Escorts and Cortinas were the most popular police cars in Britain and were a common sight in the mirrors of other Escorts and Cortinas.

G'DAY MATE
Throughout the 1970s the Escort wasn't popular in Australia, but was loved in New Zealand and sold well throughout the decade.

Standard versions of the Escort MkI allowed those on a budget to buy a decently sized family car.

By the 1970s, Mini was a marque in its own right.

3. Mini

The Mini began its life in 1959 and was produced by the British Motor Corporation until 1968, when British Leyland took over production of the pint-sized classic until 1986. By the 1970s the Mini was on its third incarnation, and was a popular car on the roads of Britain.

The MkIII version featured larger doors than its predecessor and rubber cone suspension, and the sliding windows had been replaced with more traditional winding versions. The Mini had already gained quite a reputation as a rally car, and it was also becoming something of a media star through its continued presence in film and advertising. It's perhaps strange then that the MkIII Cooper model was not a great success. The bodyshell was heavier than on previous versions and as a result the car was relatively slow. This was reflected in the sales figures and by the time the MkIII Cooper was discontinued in 1971, only about 1500 had been built. However, this did not tarnish the overall popularity of the mini wondercar.

STATS AND FACTS

SPIES AND ROBBERS

Apart from *The Italian Job*, the Mini is perhaps most famous for being driven by Matt Damon in the 2002 movie, *The Bourne Identity*.

CLASS ACT

The Mini was the original classless car, with everybody from students to pop stars buying them. The more well-heeled invariably spent fortunes customising theirs.

4. Morris Marina

Built by the Morris division of British Leyland, the Marina was one of the most popular cars in Britain during the 1970s. However, it suffered from reliablity and rust problems. The design was somewhat uninspiring and early models were beset with understeer problems because of suspension issues. These were corrected and by 1975 a MkII edition had been unveiled. Production of the Marina lasted for ten years and more than 800,000 units were produced.

• STATS AND FACTS •

AN ITALIAN MAKEOVER
Despite flagging sales, British Leyland rebadged the Marina as the Ital and kept producing it until 1984, proving that an old dog could indeed learn new tricks.

A VERY BRITISH CAR
The Marina has been described as one of the worst cars ever made, but in the period it was one of the most popular new cars in the UK.

5. Vauxhall Viva

The Viva HC was produced between 1970 and 1979, during which time some 640,000 units were built. The previous HB version had featured 'Coke-bottle' lines, but the HC reverted to the more austere box shape. The Viva was reasonably priced and cheap to run, which made it a popular choice for both families and fleet car operators. A high performance version, the Firenza, was built in 1972, which helped to keep the Viva in the public eye and contributed to its success.

• STATS AND FACTS •

SPEEDY SALES
When the Viva HC was released it became the fastest selling Vauxhall ever sold in the UK. The car, however, was not so quick.

A VIVA BY ANY OTHER NAME
In Canada, the Viva HC was known as the Firenza and marketed as a Pontiac/Buick, not a Vauxhall. This was and still is a common sales practice.

6. Austin Allegro

Produced by British Leyland, wearing Austin badges, between 1973 and 1983 the Allegro was plagued with so many problems that it was known as the 'All-aggro'. Its design was so poor that it was said to be more aerodynamic going backwards than forwards. Despite this, over 640,000 units were produced. 1975 saw the release of the Allegro II, followed by a third version in 1979. By 1980, the increasingly obsolete Allegro had fallen out of the UK's top ten sellers.

• STATS AND FACTS •

THE TEST OF TIME
In 2008 there were still 1,000 Allegros registered with the DVLA, 25 years after production had ceased, despite its terrible reputation.

AN UNDESIRABLE TITLE
In July 2008, a poll in the *Sun* newspaper branded the Allegro 'the worst car ever made', although more than 640,000 people had bought one new.

As well as the saloon, the Marina was also offered in coupé and estate forms.

The Viva HC didn't look as distinctive as its HB forebear, but it sold very well.

Many accused the Allegro of looking like an upturned bathtub, but it still sold well.

The 1100/1300 was offered by five separate BMC marques.

7. BMC 1100/1300

The BMC 1100/1300 was succeeded by the Austin Allegro and, as its name suggests, it was available in two versions; 1100cc and 1300cc. Based on the original ADO16 design, the Morris version of this plucky little car showed how incredibly enduring the idea had been. By the end of its life, the Morris 1100/1300 had been utterly surpassed by the Ford Cortina, but two decades after its release it was still a common sight on Britain's roads. Unfortunately, although it was successful, it highlighted the problems with the British motor industry, which was, by now, like the AD016 design, in its final death-throes.

• STATS AND FACTS •

GOING OUT IN STYLE
The last version of the AD016 to be built in Britain was the Vanden Plas luxury version, which rolled off the production line in June 1974.

RETIRING TO THE SUN
Production ended in Britain in 1974, but the last of the AD016 line to be produced worldwide was the Austin Apache, built in South Africa until 1977.

The Avenger was ordinary, which was part of its appeal.

8. Hillman Avenger

The Avenger was released in 1970, and was produced until 1976, when it was renamed the Chrysler Avenger. This was the first as well as the last car to be produced by Rootes after the company was taken over by Chrysler in 1967. The Avenger was similar in style to the MkIII Cortina and Vauxhall Viva, and was widely admired for its handling capabilities and ride comfort. In 1978, Chrysler went into bankruptcy and was bought by Peugeot. The Avenger was rebadged as the Talbot Avenger, but by that time Volkswagen's Golf and Vauxhall's Astra had already outclassed it.

• STATS AND FACTS •

IT'S JUST NOT CRICKET
Over 750,000 Avengers were eventually built and many were exported to America, where they were badged as the Plymouth Cricket.

VIKING AVENGER
In mainland Europe, Scandinavia was also a popular destination for the Avenger, where the Sunbeam badge was used.

American buyers got the Mustang; Europeans got the Capri.

The Arrow range, represented here by the Humber Sceptre.

9. Ford Capri

In 1969, the Capri was introduced, with Ford marketing it as the European version of its Mustang. The Capri was affordable and available with a wide range of engines, guaranteeing success. Facelifted in 1972, by 1973 it had notched up a healthy 233,000 sales. 1973 saw the MkII version released, but it was more suited to everyday driving than speed. Ford released a John Player Special edition in 1975, named after the Formula 1 team, and featuring gold pin-striping as well as gold wheels. Before the decade was out Ford released a MkIII version, but it failed to halt the decline in sales.

• STATS AND FACTS •

A DODGY GEEZER
Del Boy owned the most famous Ford Capri in Britain in the sitcom, *Only Fools and Horses*. He even kept it when he eventualy became a millionaire.

THE HELL HE DID
In the movie *Brannigan*, John Wayne famously jumped London's Tower Bridge in a Ford Capri, while chasing a MkII Jaguar.

10. Arrow Range

The Arrow was the name given to a range of cars produced under the auspices of the Rootes Group and highlights the mess that the British motor industry was in during the 1970s. The Rootes Group practised badge engineering on a massive scale; the Arrow range was the same car, wearing a multitude of different badges. The platform was variously known as the Chrysler Hunter, Hillman Minx, Hillman Hunter, Humber Sceptre and Singer Vogue, to name but a few. The most prolific seller in the range was the Hillman Hunter, which competed well with the Ford Cortina and Morris Marina.

• STATS AND FACTS •

MULTIPLE PERSONALITIES
The Rootes Arrow range is one of the most badge-engineered cars in history. Some 19 versions of the car were made in total.

HUNTING ARROWS
The Hillman Hunter was the most popular version of the Arrow. The GLS version was the most successful and is highly sought after today.

The 1275GT was a spiritual successor to the Cooper, but didn't capture the imagination in the same way.

Minis and Superminis

The rise of motoring in the 1960s opened the door for new innovations during the following decade, but trouble in the Middle East was to change the way cars were regarded by the general public and contributed to the increase in popularity of the small car.

By the start of the 1970s the Mini was firmly ensconced as the small car of choice. It was the first real supermini and had cornered the market in its class, leaving the competition trailing in its wake. Part of the problem was how to make a small car that was inexpensive to buy actually turn a profit. Ford had famously tried to reverse engineer the Mini and when it had finally succeeded, it couldn't make the car work financially. In response it pressed ahead with the Cortina, which became one of the bestselling cars of all time. Ford was to rectify this during the last part of the decade, with the release of its Fiesta, but during the 1970s one of the biggest car manufacturers in the world was predominantly out of the small car game and as a result any competition that the Mini would face would be easier to deal with.

In 1969, British Leyland released the Mini Clubman. It differed from the classic Mini in regard to its nose, which became squarer, but otherwise it was essentially the same beast. The Clubman gave birth to the fastest Mini of the 1970s, and the first true supermini – the **1275GT**. In 1972, British Leyland stopped producing the Cooper S, which carried the same 1275cc engine, leaving the 1275GT as the king of speed. The little car could go from 0–60 in 12 seconds and bottom out

Ford famously tried to reverse engineer the Mini, but they couldn't make it work financially

With its 1275cc engine, the 1275GT was effectively a facelifted Cooper S.

at 90mph. Both these figures may not seem that impressive today, but for a car that was essentially a go-kart with a roof it was very impressive indeed. The 1275GT was the first car to be produced with run-flat tyres, something that, to this day, is not universally applauded, but these stiff-walled tyres contributed to the car's lively ride. By the time production ceased, in 1980, over 110,000 1275GTs had been produced and the little car could retire knowing that during the 1970s no other small car could touch it for pace.

In 1973 the Middle East oil crisis sent shockwaves through the car industry. Since the 1960s cars had been getting bigger, both in terms of engine size and vehicle dimensions, but now it was apparent that big equalled expensive so it's no surprise that the Mini became one of the bestselling cars of the decade. Thankfully the oil crisis didn't last very long, but the writing was now on the wall and manufacturers began in earnest to design new, smaller and more fuel-efficient cars. The problem was that this took time. It wasn't possible to produce a new car overnight, as it had to be designed, built, tested and marketed before it could be released.

The Imp was introduced in 1963, but would survive until half-way through the 1970s, despite its reputation for fragility.

The only other British small car of any real note during the 1970s was the **Hillman Imp**, a car whose roots lay in the previous oil crisis of 1956 in Suez. Following the Suez problem manufacturers had sought a car that would be fuel-efficient and economical to run. Accordingly, the Rootes Group set up the Apex project and with the financial help of the British government a factory was set up in Linwood, near Paisley, to produce the new car. It was the first car factory in Scotland for over 30 years and the Imp still holds a special place in the country's history.

On 2 May 1963, the Duke of Edinburgh drove the first Imp off the production line. Hopes were high that at last there was a car that could challenge the dominance of the Mini. But it would be problems with British industry that would stifle the Imp's potential, as well as its reputation for unreliability. During the 1970s British manufacturing was in serious decline and the car industry was no different. In 1964, Chrysler had bought out Rootes, but even its financial muscle could not halt the slide, and in 1976 production of the Imp came to an end. Some 440,000 had been produced between 1963 and 1976, but those numbers were not going to threaten the

The only other British small car of any real note during the 1970s was the Hillman Imp

The Renault 5 was a true great; fun to drive, practical and spacious, plus affordable too.

Renault 5 GTL 1300

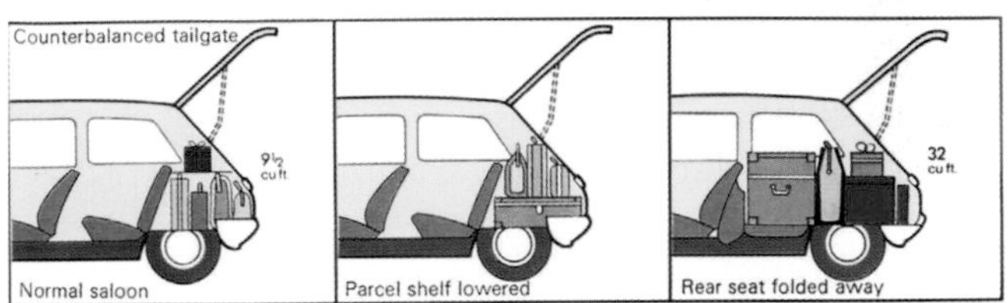

Mini. When it's considered that the Imp had many variants, and was produced by several manufacturers under the Rootes name, it stands as a case study for all that was wrong with the British car industry.

The British producers may have been struggling to find a successful small car, but their European and American cousins were having more success. Renault had unveiled its **Renault 5** in 1971, to general acclaim. It just missed out on the prestigious European Car of the Year award in 1973, and it sold well right across Europe. To compete with the Mini 1275GT, Renault developed a hot-hatch version of the 5. The Alpine, known as the **Renault 5 Gordini** in Britain (Sunbeam owned the Alpine moniker), was shipped with distinctive alloy wheels, sportier suspension and a 1.4-litre engine. Released in 1976,

MINIS/SUPERMINIS OF THE 70S

1. Mini 1275GT
2. Hillman Imp
3. Renault 5
4. Renault 5 Gordini
5. Vauxhall Chevette
6. Ford Fiesta

The Chevette's hatchback design was novel when it was introduced.

Most 1970s hatchbacks were front-wheel drive, but unusually the Chevette's power went to the rear wheels.

the Gordini was capable of achieving a top speed of 104mph and going from 0–60 in just under ten seconds. This made it quicker on paper than the 1275GT, but it didn't have the charisma of the Mini, or the handling, and was not a great success in the UK. In international competition it also struggled to beat the Mini and didn't manage to achieve a win in the infamous Monte Carlo Rally.

Vauxhall also entered the small car market with its **Chevette**. Manufactured in the UK from 1975, the car sold well in the UK, thanks in part to its practicality; between 1975 and 1978 it was the bestselling hatchback in the country and offered a slightly larger alternative to the standard small car. But despite the efforts of Vauxhall, Fiat and Peugeot, the biggest threat to the Mini was the **Ford Fiesta**. Sales began in the UK during

The Fiesta was the first front-wheel drive car to be made by Ford, and would go on to become an icon.

Despite the efforts of Vauxhall, Fiat and Peugeot, the biggest threat to the Mini was the Ford Fiesta

1976, and a basic 1-litre model could be bought for £1,856. The car was an instant success and over a million were produced by the middle of 1979. Within a couple of years the XR2 had appeared and, when it did, it would change the way that superminis were regarded and usurp the Mini as Britain's favourite small car.

The 1970s was a troubled time for car manufacturers. British makers struggled and foreign manufacturers began to take larger slices of the UK market. Car development is an evolutionary process and the 1970s taught manufacturers several lessons that would be well learnt and lead to a new generation of superminis during the 1980s. The Ford Fiesta would be at the head of this new generation.

Oiling the wheels of change

The British car industry in the 1970s was, to a large degree, mirrored by the state of the country in general. The fabric of Britain was changing and there were dark times ahead; waves of strikes swept across the country, working practices struggled to reform and British industry found it hard to compete with the powerful European Union and the might of American manufacturing muscle. But as the UK car companies gasped for air, there was another change taking place that was to influence the design and form of production cars for decades, and still does to this day.

Crisis in the Middle East

In 1973, the West found itself in the grip of an oil crisis. Frustrated at American support for Israel during the Yom Kippur War, the leading Arab members of OPEC initiated an oil embargo, forcing prices up and highlighting the West's reliance on fossil fuels. The country most affected by the embargo was the USA, but in Western Europe the knock-on effect was still severe and the motor industry was one of the hardest hit. Despite the taxation of fuel by the British and European governments, the economic revival of the 1960s had seen car sizes increasing. The lure of the motorway and influences of the American market had encouraged manufacturers to build ever bigger and more powerful models, which were now under threat of failing. The car had become a status symbol, but

Top: The oil crisis meant many garages ran out of fuel.
Centre: British citizens got used to queuing for everything.
Bottom: Production lines ground to a halt; this is Ford's.

the car's new-found position of prestige could not continue if the cost of fuel continued to rise.

The oil crisis proved to be a stark reminder to the motor industry of how reliant it was on something that was beyond its control. It forced a collective rethink and the industry began a steady move away from large models towards a new style of car – the hatchback. In the early 1970s, hatchbacks accounted for a very small percentage of the total car market, but by the end of the decade all that had changed. Another consequence of the oil crisis was the imposition of short-term speed restrictions, which saw the motorway maximum speed fall to 50mph. Fast and powerful cars were not so attractive in a world where driving quickly was outlawed and petrol costs were steadily rising. Accordingly, models such as the Ford Fiesta, Vauxhall Astra, Mini and Renault 5 were commonplace. They were economical, reliable and sporty and not seen as opulent, vulgar and a waste of the world's natural resources.

Small is the new big

Cars have to some degree always been a status symbol; an object of desire, where speed is sexy and bigger is better. But the realities of 1973 were so ingrained in the conscience of the motor trade, as well as the consumer, that the trend for smaller, more economical cars has never really left the British psyche. In current times we are experiencing a similar rise in the cost of oil and the frequent price rises are unlikely to end. Fossil fuels are running out and as they become scarcer, prices will undoubtedly rise. Today, this fact coupled with a realisation of the damage to the environment that fossil fuels are causing, has meant that we are still seeing the motoring legacies of the 1970s – and, 40 years on, the Ford Fiesta, Vauxhall Astra and the Mini are still the kings of the road.

Top: Petrol rationing led to large queues at the pumps.
Centre: Nationwide strikes gripped the motor industry.
Bottom: These strikes brought the car industry to its knees.

Saloon Cars

Over the previous decade cars had been getting larger and by the start of the 1970s the saloon had come of age. Several manufacturers competed for dominance, but ultimately this would lead to the rise of a German giant and a new style of car – the executive saloon.

Saloons have always been popular cars, but they have changed in nature somewhat over the years. Whereas previously the saloon had been the standard car, for those lucky enough to afford a car at all, by the 1970s they were more appealing to families as well as company car drivers. They offered power, space and comfort and also carried a certain amount of status, as they had an obvious presence on the roads.

The bestselling car of the 1970s was by far **Ford's Cortina**. It was the king of the saloon car and loved by businessmen and families alike. But Ford was also producing another model that would go on to become a success. The **Ford Granada** was larger than the Cortina and was aimed at the mass market as a roomy and powerful car that offered that little bit more than its younger sibling. The Granada

It's one of the most recognisable shapes of the 1970s – the MkIII Cortina.

For those wanting some luxury on a relative budget, Ford offered its Granada, seen here in MkI form.

arrived on the scene during March 1972 as a replacement for the Zephyr. Fleet hire companies that leased cars to the travelling businessman, as well as police forces and taxi operators across the country, immediately took it up, in considerable numbers. It was also popular as a hearse and a limousine. Engine sizes ranged from the basic 2-litre version through to a powerful 3-litre edition. The car was available in either a two-door or four-door variant, although the two-door was not available in the UK.

The original design of the Granada incorporated the distinctive and popular Coke-bottle lines, but in 1977 Ford updated the model and the revised version dropped the American-influenced style for straighter lines and a more aggressive image. The MkII was not produced for long in the UK and those that were bought in the country had been built in Germany. The Granada went on to be sold in the UK until 1995, but by then it had started to suffer as a change in buying trends had seen more premium marques, like BMW and Audi, preferred to more mainstream makes such as Ford.

It could only be a 70s interior with all this brown velour. This is the masterpiece that was the Granada Ghia.

One of the first compact executive cars was the BMW 02-Series, seen here in 2002 model guise.

BMW made luxury saloons in the 1950s, then moved to smaller cars. It didn't give up on big cars altogether though, as this 3.3 Li shows.

In 1968 BMW launched its **02 saloon** – one of the first luxurious and powerful small cars. The German company had already had some success with its Neu-Klasse, but it was the 02-Series that really catapulted the company onto the trajectory of success that it enjoys today. At the time of the 02's release BMW was not a company in particularly good shape, but this one car changed all that. It recreated the pre-war era of BMW success and in 1970 it won the Nurburgring 24-hour race, ensuring that racing pedigree would back up the car's potential. But it's not so much the 02 itself that changed the face of saloon cars in the 1970s, but rather its evolutionary result – the 3-Series.

The **E21 3-Series** was first shown to the public at the Olympic Stadium, in Munich, during 1975. The car shared similarities with the 2002, but it was a more driver-orientated car. The dashboard and instrument panel angled towards the driver and all the sharp and harsh edges inside the car were rounded off, giving a feeling of safety and comfort. The car was much smaller than Ford's Granada and was initially only available as a two-door variant. It was rewriting the rules for a saloon car. No longer did a saloon have to be big, it simply had to be used for a certain purpose and the German manufacturer was not idle in building upon the 3-Series' initial success.

In 1977 BMW showed off its new engine range that introduced the now famous straight-six. With the new powerplant the car continued to excel and by 1981, just six years after the car's introduction, the one millionth 3-Series drove off the production line. It had succeeded in making the saloon car sporty

BMW was not in good shape, but the 2002 saloon changed all that

Audi sold few of its cars in the UK in the 1960s and 1970s, but later on it would become a big player. This is an 80 B1.

and desirable. No longer did they have to be big and ungainly cars with powerful engines that disguised their aesthetic inadequacies. In Britain, people were bowled over by the new car. Consumers began to prefer the low spec 3-Series, as well as its German brothers and sisters, to the high-spec Fords and Vauxhalls, forcing these companies to think again. But BMW would not have things all to itself for long.

The **Audi 80 B1** went into production in 1972 and sold well in Europe. By 1978 the model had been supplanted by the B2, but nevertheless by that time over 1.1 million had been produced and it had won the European Car of the Year award, in 1973. The B2 continued where the B1 had left off and was an improvement on the earlier version. The B2 looked more modern and upmarket and it spawned the Coupé and Quattro variants that were to be so popular during the 1980s.

SALOON CARS OF THE 70S

1. Ford Cortina
2. Ford Granada
3. BMW 2002
4. BMW E21 3-Series
5. Audi 80 B1
6. Mercedes W123

Mercedes were slower to react to the new trend in saloons and didn't release their own version, the **W123**, until 1976. However, it was an instant hit and by the 1990s, it had helped lead to the venerable C-Class. The release of the W123 completed the triumvirate of German manufacturers that would dominate the executive saloon range for decades. They wouldn't have it all their own way and there were certainly pretenders to the crown, but the German manufacturers had sensed a change in the market and reacted first. While the British carmakers floundered in endless strikes and Luddite working practices, the big European manufacturers were concentrating on the larger family car or the hatchback. Ford had so much success with the Cortina and then the Escort that it was too preoccupied to really pay attention to the prevailing preferences of the public, something which ultimately led to the demise of the Granada.

It's no coincidence that BMW largely controls the executive saloon market today. The 3-Series is as popular in the Emirates and the United States as it is in Germany or Britain. The executive saloon not only became a car class in its own right, but also became the only saloon that really mattered and, as prices became more affordable, few consumers would look elsewhere.

The Mercedes W123 came in stylish coupé form, as here.

The W123 was also offered in saloon and estate guises, the latter offering tremendous practicality.

The Jaguar XJS followed in the footsteps of the iconic XK120, launched almost 30 years earlier and seen here in coupé form.

Luxury Cars

German manufacturers revolutionised the saloon car market during the 1970s, with the introduction of executive models. Luxury cars were to follow as power and speed were combined with opulence. Mercedes and Jaguar would lead the way and the luxury car would enjoy a new lease of life.

The oil crisis of the 1970s had a profound effect on the mass-produced section of the new car market, but this new-found conservatism didn't necessarily apply to the upper echelons of the luxury segment, although it did have an effect. As car ownership continued to increase at a ferocious rate, high-end cars became more and more popular and allowed manufacturers such as Jaguar and Mercedes to carve out a new niche that would bring them success and ensure their survival. These cars were in a league of their own and could survive the conservative revolution that was occuring in the family and supermini markets. The British may have been failing when it came to mass-market cars, but they still knew how to build the luxury models.

One of the key makers in the sector during the 1970s was Jaguar. Its E-Type had been a very successful car, but the time had come to update it and the XJS was chosen as the successor. The **XJS** shows how the larger sports cars of the 1960s were evolving into more luxury marques, as Porsche, Ferrari and Lamborghini took the traditional sports car in a different direction. That is not to say that the XJS wasn't fast; it was. Despite its weight, the XJS could reach 60mph from a standstill in just 7.5 seconds and was capable of a top speed of 143mph. But it suffered from being a model that was in transition and consequently became neither one thing nor the other. The car was luxurious, but perhaps for some, not luxurious enough. Jaguar's decision to market the XJS as the replacement for the classic E-Type led to calls that the car wasn't sporty enough either. With the oil crisis raging it wasn't easy for Jaguar to justify the 5.3-litre V12 engine, which also didn't help with sales figures.

'The car is the closest thing we can create to something that is alive' Sir William Lyons, co-founder of Jaguar

Buyers were slow to accept the XJS, which as far as they were concerned wasn't a worthy successor to the E-Type.

Part of the problem with the XJS's acceptance was the styling; it wasn't lithe like a Jaguar should be.

Despite these problems the XJS continued production well into the 1990s and lapped up the limelight in television programmes such as *The New Avengers* and *Return of the Saint*, ensuring that the public recognised it was a desirable luxury car.

Jaguar also had other models that fell into the luxury car category. The **XJ** and its more opulent version, the Sovereign, were also flying the flag of British class and style. Released in 1969, the XJ Series 1 was an immediate success. Between 1969 and its eventual demise in 1992 there were three different Series released, although the Series 1 remained the definitive edition. Initially available with either a 2.8 or 4.2-litre straight-six, the XJ later got the 5.3-litre V12, in 1972. Between 1968 and 1973 some 82,000 units were produced, leading to the inevitable upgrade in 1973. Unfortunately, the Series II had a reputation for poor build quality, which Jaguar rectified at the end of the decade when it asked Pininfarina to design the Series III, with stunning results. The Series III incorporated developments such as cruise control and a sunroof and went on to be the most successful of the XJ series, selling 132,952 units.

> 'Oh Lord, won't you buy me a Mercedes-Benz. My friends all drive Porsches, I must make amends'
>
> Janis Joplin

Jaguar was finding its feet again during the 1970s and it had to find them quickly as there was some serious competition. Mercedes had missed the boat in the saloon market during the decade and had been eclipsed by BMW's 3-Series, but in 1973 it released the **W116 S-Class**. Worldwide the W116 achieved a total production of 473,035 and spawned a series that is still available today.

The Mercedes S-Class, seen here in W116 form, was acknowledged as the world's best car.

Nobody could have guessed just what a phenomenon the 5-Series would become for BMW.

This first edition of the 5-Series was known as the E12 generation. It came in saloon form only.

The **S-Class** effortlessly combined style, power and safety to create one of the best luxury cars of the decade. Every aspect of the car, from the headrests to the rain gutters, was intended to make the S-Class safe and it was one of the first cars available with airbags and ABS. The most powerful model was the 450SE, which was awarded the European Car of the Year, in 1974, although there was a limited edition 450 SEL 6.9 model also released. Mercedes took great care over the design of its engines, thereby minimising the effect of the oil crisis. In 1979, the W126 replaced the W116 and brought aerodynamic improvements as well as lighter engine blocks that allowed power to be increased without the usual weight penalty. The W126 S-Class was the first luxury car to win the Australian Car of the Year award in 1981, ensuring its place at the top of the luxury class pile.

LUXURY CARS OF THE 70S

1. Jaguar XJS and XJ6
2. Mercedes S-Class W116
3. BMW 5-Series
4. Range Rover
5. Aston Martin V8 Vantage

BMW kept the pressure on during the 1970s with its **5-Series** range, which saw it further develop its status as a quality manufacturer. The 5-Series was bigger than the 3-Series and offered more comfort, power and luxury. Available in either a 520 or 520i variant initially, by 1975 the 525 had been added to the range, which sported a six-cylinder engine producing 165bhp. The E12 5-Series was popular, but it was really a stepping stone for the second-generation 5-Series, the E28, released in 1982.

During the 1970s another class of luxury car had its beginnings. The **Range Rover** was released in 1970 and initially wasn't intended as a luxury 4x4. It was meant to compete in

The Range Rover launched a whole new genre of luxury SUVs – way back in 1970.

The Aston Martin V8 Vantage was one of the world's greatest grand tourers, but it was costly and thirsty.

The Aston Martin V8 Vantage could achieve speeds of 170mph

the standard 4x4 market, although it was certainly an improvement on the rugged Land Rover. By the time of the second-generation Range Rover, in the early 1990s, the marque had achieved luxury status and the development of the vehicle over the years paved the way for future luxury 4x4s, such as the BMW X5 and the Mercedes ML range.

The luxury car had come a long way since the beginning of the 1960s. Jaguar and Mercedes had risen to the top of the pile, but there were others gaining ground, quickly. 1977 saw the release of the **Aston Martin V8 Vantage**, which could achieve speeds of 170mph and although it was branded as a sports car, it offered far more in the way of luxury than its competitors.

By the end of the decade, luxury cars varied from 4x4s to sports cars and upmarket saloons. The luxury car class was growing and evolving, enabling it to embrace an ever wider audience. Over the following decades as cars got more powerful and further refined, the luxury car would continue to go from strength to strength and previously unimaginable levels of car design would soon be achieved.

The Lamborghini Countach is arguably the most dramatic car ever produced in any quantity.

Sports Cars

After the heady days of the 1960s, in the 70s sports car manufacturers were forced into a period of reflection, redesign and restriction. The 70s was an era of price rises at the petrol pumps, economic slump and rising environmental concerns. All of this did not bode well for the sports car but despite these restricting factors it was a decade that saw the inception of some truly iconic cars. The Lamborghini Countach, Lotus Esprit Turbo and Jaguar's XJ12 and XJS all arrived during the decade, as well as new versions of old classics, such as the Porsche 911 Turbo.

Lamborghini was already a well-regarded manufacturer thanks to its impressive Miura and in 1971, at the Geneva Motor Show, it was propelled into the stratosphere with the release of the **Countach**. It took a further three years for the car to be available to buy, due

Some of the greatest cars ever conceived were built during the 1970s. Technology and car design took a giant leap towards modernity, giving birth to classics such as the Porsche 911 Turbo and the Lamborghini Countach. Sports cars were about to become supercars.

‘You buy a Ferrari when you want to be somebody. You buy a Lamborghini when you are somebody’
Frank Sinatra

to production issues and engine problems. When it finally reached the showrooms of London, Paris, Monaco and Rome it was fitted with a 3.9-litre V12 that rocketed the car to a top speed of 175mph, and possessed an impressive 0–60 time of just 5.7 seconds. The Countach's most distinctive feature was its scissor doors, which opened upwards. They made it difficult to enter and exit the car, but they differentiated it from the crowd

The Lotus Esprit had the looks of a Lamborghini Countach, but came at a much lower cost.

and gave it a unique selling point. The original model was usurped, in 1978, when it was replaced with an S version that featured wider wheels and a large rear spoiler. The Countach continued to be produced throughout the 1970s and 80s, until production ceased in July 1990, by which time it was one of the most famous and sought after cars in the world.

While the Countach wowed crowds around the world, Colin Chapman's company, Lotus, was busy in Britain creating its own version of the sports car. The result was the **Espirt Turbo**, a mid-engined supercar that was unveiled at the 1975 London Motor Show. On release, the Esprit didn't have the performance of the Countach, but it did have the looks. In fact, it was such a beautiful looking car that it soon became a movie star. The 1977 release of the James Bond film, *The Spy Who Loved Me*, did more for sales of the car than anything to do with its performance statistics. Allegedly Colin Chapman, having been tipped off that the new Bond film was shooting at Pinewood Studios, drove a production model of the Esprit S1 to the studios and parked it on the lot. It didn't take long for it to catch the eye of Cubby Broccoli, and the rest is history. The film ensured that the Esprit became a huge seller, with waiting lists several years long, although it's not known how many owners discovered, to their cost and embarrassment, that it was only in the movie that the car could change into a submarine!

In 1975, production of the now legendary E-Type finally came to an end. It was replaced by the **Jaguar XJS**, a car that, strictly speaking, was more of a GT (Grand Tourer) than a sports car. The 1970s saw further development of the GT, largely as a result of the oil crisis of 1973 and the growing concern over the safety and environmental side effects of the sports car. Between 1975 and 1986 Jaguar produced some 115,413 units of the XJS and

SPORTS CARS OF THE 70S

1. Lamborghini Countach
2. Lotus Esprit Turbo
3. Jaguar XJS
4. Jaguar XJ12
5. BMW 3-Series
6. Porsche 911 Turbo

it too featured in many films and television programmes throughout its life such as *Columbo*, *The Saint*, *Knots Landing*, *Dallas* and *Falcon Crest*. The XJS proved that fast cars did not have to be small and noisy two-seaters. They could offer class, comfort and style as well as impressive speed and acceleration.

This idea of a fast, powerful and comfortable car was not unique to the XJS. Jaguar also produced the **XJ12**, which was to become the most popular 12-cylinder four-seater in the world. Born from developments in the E-Type and XJ6, the XJ12 was unveiled by Jaguar in 1972. It produced 309bhp, could reach a top speed of 147mph and touch 60mph in 7.4 seconds from a standing start. These statistics made the XJ12 the fastest four-seat car in the world and a worthy competitor to the more traditional sports cars of Lotus, Porsche and Lamborghini.

It didn't take long for it to catch the eye of Cubby Broccoli, and the rest is history

Events in the Middle East had a damaging effect on developments in the world of sports cars. Paradoxically, this helped lead to cars like the Jaguar XJS and XJ12, but it almost

At first the Jaguar XJS came with V12 power only, but in time there would also be six-cylinder versions.

The Porsche 911 – photgraphed here in 1974 – continued to develop throughout the 70s.

finished off another important development in fast car design, the turbocharger. In 1973, BMW released its developmental 2002 Turbo at the Frankfurt Motor Show. The 2002 was a striking-looking car. It had no front bumper; instead there was a masculine-looking spoiler with the word 'Turbo' printed on it in reverse script, so that drivers could read the word in their rear view mirror when the 2002 screeched up behind them. In the era of the petrol crisis this was seen as irresponsible and was soon removed by the manufacturer, although this didn't stop owners buying their own stickers. Indeed, the whole car was seen as irresponsible and as a result it only remained in production for ten months, with just 1,672 of them ever made. The car suffered from notorious turbo lag and as it

> 'I couldn't find the sports car of my dreams, so I built it myself'
>
> Ferdinand Porsche

was capable of achieving 0–60 in under 7 seconds and had a top speed of 130mph, it was also fairly scary to drive. The fact that the 2002 Turbo didn't last long is not really the point. It set the scene for **BMW's 3-Series** and showed what a turbocharger could do to the performance of a car. The oil crisis couldn't last forever, but the turbo was here to stay.

Porsche has always offered the 911 in a multitude of forms, with various engine, transmission and bodystyle options.

In 1974, just one year after the oil crisis had begun, Porsche adapted its bestselling car to create the **911 Turbo**, propelling it from a desirable car into the most famous German sports car in the world. In 1962, the original 911 had a top speed of 130mph, but the addition of the turbo meant that the car could now do an eye-watering 153mph and hit 100mph from zero in just 14 seconds. Taking a cue from Jaguar, the 911 Turbo had comforts, such as air conditioning and electric windows, fitted as standard. In 1978, the engine size was increased to 3.3 litres, pushing the top speed to 160mph and shaving two seconds off the 0–100mph time. The 911 Turbo was so successful that it was another ten years until the engine design radically changed.

In an era of conservatism it seems odd that the turbo even saw the light of day, but it was a development that would have long-lasting consequences for the car. It showed that in the upper echelons of car development, concerns over fuel prices played second fiddle to the desire for speed and performance. Sports cars didn't have to abide by the same rules as production cars. As a result, the future cars, that the lesser mortals amongst us were destined to drive, would benefit from great leaps in racing technology and development. But, ironically, while these early turbocharged cars were costly performance models, in time the turbocharger would be used for greater economy.

1980s

DMC

10 Bestsellers

The 1980s witnessed sweeping changes in British society. 'Thatcher's Britain' was a time of economic boom, where excesses of personal consumption were commonplace. The love affair with the hatchback continued, but a new type of car was becoming common on the roads of Britain. It was the sports car and everybody seemed to want one.

Largely driven by stars of American television programmes, such as *Miami Vice*, cars like the Ferrari Testarossa and the Porsche 911 Turbo were seen as the ultimate status symbols. The new breed of young upwardly mobile professionals (YUPPIEs) couldn't get enough of them and powerful cars began to make a resurgence as the decade unfolded.

The 1980s saw the appearance of more and more foreign manufacturers in the UK, both in terms of the cars on the road and the factories in the towns and cities. In 1986 Nissan became the first Japanese manufacturer to set up production facilities in the UK, opening a plant in Sunderland. It didn't take long for the likes of Honda and Toyota to join it.

This foreign influx increasingly marginalised the few remaining British manufacturing companies, which were already struggling to survive. In the mid-80s British Leyland sought government help to develop the Mini Metro, Maestro and Montego and was renamed the Rover Group. These cars were to prove very popular, but they were also to be the last of a dying breed. The writing was on the wall and the 1980s was to sound the deathknell for British car production.

of the 1980s

1.

• STATS AND FACTS •

ACROSS THE POND

In the United States of America the Escort name was applied to several different Ford models, but all of them were different from the UK versions of the bestselling car.

BRENDA

The Ford Escort was codenamed 'Brenda' during its development. Although, rather wisely, Ford decided not to keep the name upon the car's release.

Ford Escort buyers could choose from hatchback, estate or cabriolet bodystyles, or even a saloon in the shape of the Orion.

Ford Escort

The 1980s belonged to Ford. Throughout the 1970s it had three cars in the top 10 bestseller list, but during the 1980s this increased to five. Sitting at the top of the tree and ensuring Ford's domination of the new-car market, was the Escort.

The MkIII Escort was unveiled in September 1980 to the advertising tagline of 'Simple is Efficient'. The car was intended to compete with the Volkswagen Golf, a growing favourite on the roads of Britain. However, The MkIII Escort was not received well by critics. Due to the positive camber bias on the front wheels, the Escort's ride could be unforgiving and the shock absorbers were not able to cope with how the the car was set up.

Despite these initial problems, the new Escort built on the popularity of the MkII. New features, which in later years were to become standard on almost every car, adorned the MkIII. These included warning lights for low fuel, oil and screen wash. Central locking and electric windows were also available as extras, bringing luxuries to the mass market.

When, in 1986, the MkIV Escort was released, it was essentially an updated MkIII, as opposed to a brave new model, but there was little point in changing a winning formula; the availability of anti-lock brakes was a first for the segment. Both the MkIII and MkIV were available in the XR3 format, so beloved by boy racers across the country. The XR3 models featured such refinements as a twin-choke Weber carburettor, and when fuel injection was fitted, the now XR3i became a highly sought after model. Before the XR models came the RS1600i though; a car that's now very rare and highly sought after.

In the UK, the Ford Escort was the bestselling car of all time

Despite its overwhelming success on the roads of Britain the MkIII didn't fare well on the rally circuit. The change from rear-wheel drive to front-wheel drive didn't help matters, but the Cosworth version of the MkIV did have more success. Although this was disappointing to Ford, the sales figures were not and the Escort overtook the Cortina as the bestselling car of the 1980s, as early as 1982.

Ford was several years behind the Volkswagen Golf GTi with its hot Escort, the XR3 and XR3i.

2. Vauxhall Cavalier

Vauxhall released its spacious and practical MkII Cavalier in 1981, and it proved extremely popular with the British public, helped in no small way by the wide range of engines, trims and bodystyles on offer; there was even a convertible on the market. There were no fewer then 15 different versions of the Cavalier MkII available, with a choice of either a 1.3 or 1.6-litre engine.

In its first year the MkII Cavalier won the *What Car?* Car of the Year award, greatly aiding sales across the UK. The MkII received a facelift during 1985, which gave it a new grille, modified rear light cluster and improved upholstery. A further facelift in 1987 saw more improvements and also the introduction of the SRi 130; a 2-litre, 130bhp version that could achieve 0–60 in a swift 8 seconds.

• STATS AND FACTS •

BACK TO THE FUTURE
On its release in the 1980s Vauxhall branded the Cavalier 'The Car of the Future' due to features such as anti-lock brakes and a trip computer.

DRIVING CHANGE
With the MKII version the Cavalier switched from rear-wheel to front-wheel drive. It was an advance, but not in the eyes of everyone.

The Cavalier was a common sight on the motorways of Britain, which considering it won the Fleet Car of the Year award in 1985, 86 and 87 is not surprising. Ford's top position was under threat and Vauxhall would push it all the way over the coming years.

The convertible was always a rare version of the Cavalier; now it's the most collectible.

The Ford Fiesta provided the perfect basis for a hot hatch.

3. Ford Fiesta

The original Ford Fiesta had been released in 1976 and sold well for the first few years of the 1980s. But it was the release of the MkII version, in 1983, that cemented the car's place in motoring history. With the top tens for the 1970s and 80s dominated by larger cars, the Fiesta catered for the family and the young, and was able to compete with the Escort and the Cavalier, even though it was half their size.

The MkII was really just a MKI with a more rounded body, but it was nippy and cheap to run, appealing to the heart of the family man. The release of the XR2 version, in June 1984, was the stuff of dreams for young men looking for the thrill of speed. The car featured the same 1.6-litre engine as the XR3, which made it very quick indeed, quicker if it was given the legendary Turbo-Technics makeover. Given this, it is perhaps no surprise that 10 per cent of all MkII Fiestas sold were XR2s. Go-faster stripes, shell-suits and extra headlights also allegedly added speed.

• STATS AND FACTS •

FAST BUT NOT QUICK

The XR2 was the hot hatch of its day, but strangely not that quick, achieving 0–60 in 9.3 seconds and a top speed of 109mph.

INTERNATIONAL FIESTA

The Fiesta was a global car and has been built in Europe, Brazil, Argentina, Mexico, Venezuela, China, India, Thailand and South Africa.

4. Austin/MG Metro

British Leyland released the Metro in 1980. It would be built for the next 18 years and became a much-loved British car. In 1982, an MG version of the Metro was released and it was hoped that the car would be the saviour of British Leyland. It was the first small car of note to be released by the ageing British manufacturer since the Mini, which it was intended to replace. Initially it proved very popular, but soon began to be outsold by the Ford Fiesta.

• STATS AND FACTS •

THE EUROPEANS ARE COMING
The 1980s TV advert for the Metro depicted the car fighting foreign invaders landing on the beaches of Britain in World War II landing crafts.

BIG BROTHER
Despite its similar size, the Metro was intended as a big brother for the Mini, rather than as a replacement. Which is just as well as it could never replace the Mini.

5. Ford Sierra

Released in 1982, the Sierra was Ford's replacement for the bestselling Cortina. It was modern in appearance, but Ford cleverly kept the Cortina engines and gearboxes, so as not to alienate its client base. It was available in many varieties, ranging from the 1.3L to the smart 2.3-litre V6 Ghia. At first the Sierra couldn't match the popularity of Vauxhall's Cavalier, but with the Sapphire saloon version, in 1987, Ford began to turn things around and the Sierra went from strength to strength.

• STATS AND FACTS •

SIERRA SPEED
When the Sierra XR4i was released in 1986, it was capable of reaching 150mph, keeping traffic police around the world very busy indeed.

FUTURE STYLE
On its release, the Sierra's avant-garde styling design put off many drivers of the old Cortina. However, the 'futuristic' design served it well in the years to come.

6. Vauxhall Astra

Launched in 1980, the Astra was really a renamed Opel Kadett. It replaced the Viva and gave Volkswagen's Golf some serious competition, not so much in terms of sales, as the Golf was considerably more expensive, but certainly in terms of performance and style. The Astra GTE also gave the XR3 and Golf GTi a good run for their money, winning the prestigious *What Car?* Car of the Year award, in 1980. The Astra spawned many updated versions and is still a bestselling model today.

• STATS AND FACTS •

ASTRA-NOMICAL!
The Astra GTE 16v was capable of producing 150bhp, making it extremely powerful for its time and accordingly a very desirable car.

NUMBER CRUNCHER
The Astra GTE also sported a futuristic, LCD dashboard displaying the readout in digital numbers, as opposed to traditional dials.

In MG form, the Metro became quite a smart hatch; in Turbo guise it was quick too.

The Sierra was nicknamed the Jellymould, thanks to its curvy shape.

It was boxy and quite ordinary, but the Astra was also affordable and practical.

The Cortina was succeeded by the Sierra in 1982.

7. Ford Cortina

Despite the success of the Escort and Fiesta, the Cortina continued to sell well in its twilight years. Indeed in 1982, its final year of production, it still achieved the status of the second bestselling car in Britain – the number one being the Escort. For ten years it had held the number one spot, but times were changing and competition was growing. Despite this, the Cortina did not drive off quietly into the night. In May 1992 the *Times* newspaper declared that even though the car had not been produced for ten years it was still among the ten most common cars on the roads of Britain.

• STATS AND FACTS •

STAYING POWER
The success of the Cortina and the fact that it was still popular long after production had ceased, ensured that Ford would keep producing a larger car.

A TOUCH OF CLASS
The Cortina's name was inspired by the name of the Italian ski resort Cortina D'Ampezzo, lending a touch of class to Ford's popular car.

The Orion was nothing more than an Escort with a boot.

8. Ford Orion

Contributing to Ford's domination of the 1980s was the Orion. Between 1983 and 1993 more then 3.5 million units were sold as the car proved to be a popular saloon alternative to the hatchback Escort. The Ghia version included such refinements as central locking, sports seats, electric windows and a sunroof. The 1.6i shared the same engine with the Escort XR3i, making it a popular choice for people who wanted to avoid their insurance company's wrath. Before the decade was over, a MkII version had been released and the car helped consolidate Ford's number one status.

• STATS AND FACTS •

INJECTING PROGRESS
The Orion was especially ground-breaking family but the fitment of electronic fuel injection meant at least it was ahead of some of its rivals.

IMPRESSIVE FIGURES
A total of 3,534,239 Orions were sold throughout the car's ten-year life, showing that there was still demand for saloon cars in the era of the hatchback.

In MG form the Maestro looked sporty and went well.

9. Austin/MG Maestro

Sold between 1983 and 1994 by Austin and 1983 and 1991 by MG, the Maestro had mixed reviews, although it did sell well enough to make the UK's top ten best-seller list in the 1980s. The Maestro was a four-door hatchback designed to take on the might of the Cavalier and Sierra. It was considered a roomy, efficient and competent car and in 1986 and 1987 the Maestro sold very well, but the release of the Rover 200 in 1989 spelled the end for the Maestro. The tired working practices of its British manufacturers meant that it was functional, but never world-beating.

• STATS AND FACTS •

HAVE A WORD
The Maestro was one of the first cars to speak to the driver, using the voices of, amongst others, 1980s Dutch TV detective, Van der Valk.

FASTER THAN A FERRARI
The MG Maestro Turbo had a claimed 0–60 time of 6.7 seconds. That beat the Ferrari Mondial, which had a 0–60 time of only 7 seconds.

The Nova was the driving school's favourite in the 1980s.

10. Vauxhall Nova

The Nova represented Vauxhall's attempt at a super-mini and it proved to be very successful. The car was launched in Europe too, where it was sold as the Opel Corsa. In the UK it was known as the Nova and it proved to be a worthy competitor to the Fiesta and the Metro. Engines ranged from the basic 1.0-litre through to the sporty 1.6 GTE version, which could take on the XR2. The Nova was released in 1983 and sold well throughout the 1980s. In 1990 it was replaced with the MkII and the newest version of the Nova, now rebranded the Corsa (again), still adorns the forecourts of Vauxhall garages today.

• STATS AND FACTS •

BUILDING POPULARITY
Although loved by young men, Vauxhall aimed the Nova at young women. The TV advert showed a young woman in her Nova taking a short cut through a building site.

EURO EYES ONLY
The Nova, and its European version, the Corsa, has never been sold in America or Canada, making it a truly European car.

Minis and Superminis

By the end of the 1980s a third of the top ten bestselling cars in the UK were superminis. There had been a change in approach from the big car manufacturers, mainly due to the oil crisis of the previous decade. Small was now beautiful and the 1980s would be a defining decade for the supermini.

At the start of the 1980s the British car industry was on its last legs. British Leyland was in dire financial trouble and the release of the Austin Metro, in 1980, highlighted all that was wrong with the British car industry. It was not that the car wasn't popular, or that the British people didn't want it; it was and they did. There was a great

The Metro was intended to replace the Mini, but it was the Metro that was killed off first.

The Fiat 127 seemed like the unlikely basis for a sporty supermini, but there was one – and this was it.

deal of interest from the public when the car was launched. British Leyland ran a jingoistic advertising campaign depicting the Metro repelling the European competition, in the form of **Fiat 127s**, **Renault 5s** and **Volkswagen Polos** from the beaches of Britain, rousing British sentiments and patriotic fervour. The car proved a massive hit thanks to its economy and practicality. All this led to the Metro selling very well and for the first few years of the 1980s it was the bestselling supermini in the country.

The Austin Metro highlighted all that was wrong with the British car industry

In 1982, the **MG Metro** and the Vanden Plas version were released, taking the supermini upmarket. The Vanden Plas brought a touch of luxury to the Metro with such refinements as a cassette player and electric windows. The MG

The Fiat 127 proved a great hit across Europe, with its practicality and low purchase prices.

The VW Polo II Coupe was one of the largest models in the supermini class.

There are many who reckon the Peugeot 205 GTi was the finest hot hatch ever created, bar none.

variant was capable of speeds above 100mph and a 0–60 time of just over 10 seconds. The Turbo version of the MG Metro packed a 93bhp engine that rocketed the car to 60mph in under 9 seconds, making it a common choice with boy racers around the country. All this seeming success was reinforced with a facelift in 1985 and over the course of the 1980s the Metro sold over one million units. So, what was the problem?

The problem was that the Metro was a victim of its own success. It was an inward-looking car made by an isolated and inward-looking company. The Metro was a big seller in the UK, but it didn't sell well abroad. It may have been pictured beating back the European models from whence they came, but those European models had already conquered the rest of Europe and, had they landed, they may have taught British Leyland a thing or two. The Metro was British Leyland's first new small car in over 20 years and the Metro simply didn't embody the technological advances of its European brethren. It was a false new dawn for what was left of British car

The Citroen AX felt as though it was made of tin foil, but the lightweight bodyshell meant it was incredibly efficient.

Car magazine voted the 205 the 1980s Car of the Decade

manufacturing and although the Metro may have beaten off the invaders, it would not be able to keep them at bay.

Principal amongst the Metro's competitors was the **Peugeot 205**, a car that was the very antithesis of the Metro. The 205 was a stylish small car and is often referred to as the definitive supermini of the 1980s. Indeed, it won *What Car?* Car of the year in 1984 and *Car* magazine voted it the 1980s 'Car of the Decade'. Coincidently, it was probably the car that turned around the fortunes of Peugeot, whereas the Metro was the car that condemned British Leyland.

The 205 was launched in 1983 and in its first year it almost won the European Car of the Year award, just being beaten by

MINIS AND SUPERMINIS OF THE 80S

1. Fiat 127
2. Renault 5
3. VW Polo
4. MG Metro
5. Peugeot 205
6. Fiat Uno
7. Citroen AX
8. Vauxhall Nova
9. Ford Fiesta XR2

In Turbo form, the Fiat Uno was seriously rapid.

Most importantly the MKII gave birth to the fabulous XR2

A 1981 Renault 5 TL.

another of the European superminis, the **Fiat Uno**. The secret of the 205 was that it was a forward-thinking car. As Peugeot had not been restricted by the working practices of British Leyland it had been able to think to the future as opposed to looking back on the past. The 205 utilised modern technology, embraced better suspension systems, namely Macpherson struts at the front and a torsion bar set-up at the rear, giving the car a really comfortable ride along with plenty of boot space. The 205 was economical and cheap to run and looked at home on the streets of any European city. Between 1983 and 1998 Peugeot sold over 5.3 million 205s, dwarfing the amount of Metros sold in the same period. It was a lesson in how to build a small car, a lesson that British Leyland had not heeded.

Peugeot further improved on the 205 with the release of the now-legendary GTi versions. Available with either a 1.6 or 1.9-litre engine, the GTi offered a superlative driving experience. The GTi versions looked sporty, were very quick and offered sublime handling. In the end, it was rising insurance costs that killed the car – as with most 1980s hot hatches – but it still has a place amongst the very best superminis ever made.

The 1980s also saw the rise of the Volkswagen Polo, the **Citroen AX**, the Fiat Uno and the **Vauxhall Nova** (named the Corsa everywhere other than Britain). All these were excellent cars that sold well around the world. Although this was the case, there is one car that reigned supreme in the supermini category during the 1980s, and that was the **Fiesta**. Ford's little car had started to show its potential during the last part of the 1970s, but it was the 80s when the car really flourished.

1983 saw the release of the Fiesta MkII, a revamped version of the original. It sported new lines, a new engine and, most importantly for enthusiasts, a revised version of the fabulous XR2; one of the first superminis. It was loud, brash, fast and stood out from the crowd. It was also able to compete with the 205 GTi, and it was a runaway success. The XR2 was loved by boy racers up and down the country and during the 1980s every high street in Britain was replete with a mullet-sporting twenty-something in his go-faster striped XR2. The amazing thing about the car is that although it was quick, it was not as quick as was imagined. It also didn't have the refinements of the Vanden Plas or MG Metros. But none of this mattered. It was cool, and in the 80s that was enough.

The supermini came of age during the 1980s and as a vehicle class it would go from strength to strength. In the following decades rising insurance costs put an end to street racers like the 205 GTi and the XR2, but they showed how far the car had come from the days of the Austin 1100. While British Leyland showed with the Metro that it was stuck in a time warp, the competition seized the day and the next time it arrived in force on Britain's shores, the Metro would not be there to push it back into the sea.

The Fiesta XR2 wasn't as much fun as a 205 GTi or Golf GTi, but it was more attainable and looked every bit as fantastic.

The rise of the supercar

For those of us old enough to remember, it's impossible to forget the seemingly endless supply of American television shows that played on British screens during the 1980s. The one thing that they all had in common was that the real stars of the show were the cars, often driven at furious speeds by the drama's main protagonists. Magnum (PI) had his Ferrari 308 GTS, Michael Knight was seldom without his computerised Trans-Am (known as KITT), Face drove a 1984 Corvette in *The A-Team*, and who could forget Sonny Crockett's love for Ferraris in *Miami Vice?* Over the many series of the show he drove a Ferrari Daytona Spyder and the famous white Testarossa.

Greed is good

This American culture soon began to rub off on the people of Britain, and particularly on the new nouveau riche that Thatcher's government was creating. Showrooms for high-end marques such as Porsche, Aston Martin and Ferrari began to fill London's Mayfair and Park Lane, and no self-respecting, bouffant hair-styled city boy would be seen without his shiny suit and European sports car. The economic troubles of the previous decade seemed a distant memory, as fast and powerful cars experienced a revival, fed by the 80s culture and the notion that, as Gordon Gekko famously proclaimed, 'greed is good'.

Top: The rise of the yuppie was a major 80s phenomenon.
Centre: The Sierra 'Cossie' was one of the defining 80s cars.
Bottom: *Miami Vice* mixed music and cars to great effect.

Affordable supercars?

To the average person, Ferraris and Porsches were still out of reach, and demand increased for faster production cars. Ford released its legendary Escort XR3i at the beginning of the decade, closely followed by the Sierra Cosworth. Towards the end of the 1980s Peugeot released the 205 GTi and other European manufacturers, such as BMW, began to produce faster variants of its standard models. For those who couldn't afford these souped-up road cars, there was always the go-faster stripe, or the 'Big-Boy' exhaust to give the impression of success and status.

Not all of the cars depicted in American dramas made the crossover to British shores. In the film *Back to the Future*, Michael J Fox's character drove a gull-winged DeLorean DMC-12, a car that not only looked like the future, but also was seemingly capable of going back in time. The DeLorean proved to be strangely prescient, as the company had already gone bust by the time of the film's release, doubtless leaving them wishing that their car really could traverse the boundaries of time.

As with most developments in the motor industry, once they arrive they are usually here to stay and the legacy of the 1980s is still visible today. Most manufacturers will make a sporty and powerful version of a standard car. BMW has the M3 as the top-line 3 series, Ford has the Focus ST, and the Golf GTi still reigns supreme as the king of the hot hatches. Despite economic downturns, rising costs of fuel and the cries from campaigners that cars are damaging the environment, fast cars will always be objects of desire. Fortunately, these days, go-faster stripes and mullet hairstyles are no longer so important.

Top: The Ferrari 308 was Magnum PI's car of choice.
Centre: The DeLorean was an unmitigated disaster.
Bottom: Greed was good in the Margaret Thatcher era.

Small Family Cars

By the start of the 1980s the car market had expanded to such a degree that the family car had split into smaller and larger classes. The smaller family car proved to be popular and this resulted in new manufacturers entering the market, particularly from Japan.

The 1984 MG Maestro gave a considerably better performance than its predecessor.

British Leyland released the **Maestro** in 1983 as a flagship model for the burgeoning small family car class. It was initially well received and the first reviews were complimentary, if not a bit underwhelming. The car was roomy for its size and comfortable, and the S-Series engines that were added to the range in 1984, further improved the Maestro. There was also an MG version, rushed into service during 1983, but while it looked the part, it wasn't really up to the job. The MG was beset with problems from the start and was quickly replaced with a more advanced 2-litre version just a year later. The improved version was a much better car and could even give the Golf GTi and Escort XR3i a decent run for their money.

The problems with the Maestro were linked to issues at British Leyland. The car wasn't awful and it incorporated some nice touches, such as a laminated windscreen, voice warning system and a trip computer. But these were largely cosmetic refinements and too many mistakes were made involving the engine range, premature release of the MG variant and the lack of turbo power on the diesels. But the real issue for the Maestro was that its reputation was sullied by its association with British Leyland. The company lurched from one financial problem to the next, and when it was sold to British Aerospace in 1986 the Austin badges were dropped. The launch of the **Rover 200** in 1989 saw the Maestro relegated by the manufacturer and the MG variants were cancelled, in 1991. Ironically, the release of the Rover 200 gave the Maestro a final lease of life. The cost was reduced and it found itself competing with smaller cars, such as the Peugeot 205, which meant the Maestro could offer a lot more for the same money. In the Maestro's first full year of production it accounted for 83,000 sales and it was the bestselling car in Britain that year. But a decade later that number was down to just 7,000 sales and British Leyland's dream had died.

The MG Maestro initially featured a fuel-injected 1.6-litre engine, which was underwhelming; the later cars were much better with their 2-litre engines.

The problems with the Maestro involved the same old story for British Leyland

The MkII version of the Volkswagen Golf GTi was even better than the first, which didn't seem possible.

The Escort had the XR3i, the Astra had the GTE and the Golf the GTi

Part of the Maestro's downfall was at the hands of two outstanding cars; the Ford Escort and the Vauxhall Astra. The **MkIII Escort** not only dominated the small family car sector, but it also wiped the floor with every other car on the market. During the 1980s it was by far and away the bestselling car in the country and was everything that the Maestro was not. From the off the Escort embodied a high-tech and high-efficiency design and was a big improvement on the already successful formula. By the end of 1986 the MkIV had been released, further compounding the market position of Ford, and the car sold in huge numbers all around the world.

Ford introduced the XR3 as the sporty version of its Escort MkIII; later would come the injected XR3i edition.

The Rover 200 was little more than a rebadged Honda, just as its predecessor the Triumph Acclaim had been.

Vauxhall had similar success with its **Astra MkII**, which was released in 1984. The MkII abandoned the boxy design of its predecessor and adopted a rounder and smoother shape, leading to a victory in the European Car of the Year awards, in 1985. The MkII Astra came very close to outselling the Escort during the 1980s, and it was a worthy pretender to the throne. Volkswagen also competed for the Escort's crown with its **Golf MkII**. The MkII version came on the market at the same time as the Astra MkII and sold very well. The Golf was very well built, embodying the fundamental principles of German car design, but as a result was too expensive to trouble Ford's Escort in terms of market share.

The Escort, Astra and Golf were all very successful and worthy cars in the small family car sector of the market. But underlying this success was a common thread – the hot hatch versions of the family car. The Escort had the XR3i, the Astra the GTE and the Golf the GTi. These speedy versions of the family car massively aided the sales of their more staid

Rover 200 buyers could choose between Honda-engined 213 or Rover-engined 216 variants.

The Astra GTE was quick, and even more so by the time it had been turbocharged by Turbo Technics.

versions. Every family man who bought an Escort saw it more as an XR3i than a 1.6GL and the same went for the Golf and Astra. The pace of these hot hatch versions was blistering and they were able to compete with cars that had long been considered far sportier. As more and more investment went into the small family car, the refinements of the hot hatch would filter down to the rest of the range and the popularity of the hot hatches helped to push car design forward, making them an intrinsic part of each company's model range. This European attitude to car manufacturing helped Vauxhall, Volkswagen and Ford (which is American, but had been in the European market since the beginning) to keep one step ahead of the new kids on the block – the Japanese.

SMALL FAMILY CARS OF THE 80S

1. Austin Maestro
2. Rover 200
3. Ford Escort MkIII
4. Vauxhall Astra MkII
5. VW Golf MkII
6. Toyota Corolla
7. Honda Civic
8. Nissan Sunny

Before the 1980s the British and European car makers had been at the forefront of their domestic markets, but rampant globalisation meant all that was about to change as the might of Japanese engineering began to come to the fore. 1983 saw the fifth generation of **Toyota's Corolla** and there was a further generation released in 1987. The same was true for Honda, which produced two versions of its **Civic** during the decade. Nissan also entered the market with its revamped **Sunny**, a car that was loved by taxi firms across the UK. The Japanese cars provided something different from their European counterparts and laid the foundations for great success over the coming decades. They would experience a growing reputation for engineering excellence and reliability, and by the turn of the century they would lead the way in hybrid powertrains and modern green technology.

European models were still outselling Japanese cars by 1990, but it was clear that they were not going away. Indeed, the Honda Civic and Accord are still big sellers today and many consider the Accord to be the most reliable car ever made. After decades of having things their own way the Europeans would now have to operate in a global marketplace and this would benefit the new car buyer no end. The small family car had carved out a niche for itself and it wouldn't be long before it was one of the most popular classes of new cars around the world.

European models were still outselling the Japanese by the end of the decade

The Honda Civic has long stood for efficiency, with the car proving a big hit all around the world.

Nissan offered numerous versions of the Sunny, including this very boxy ZX coupé.

Large Family Cars

The rise in car ownership during the 1970s and 80s saw the family car market split into small and large sectors. Ford was well placed to capitalise on this as it had two bestsellers in the Escort and the Cortina, but competition would be strong between manufacturers and also between the small and large sectors.

The split into small and large versions of the family car had its roots, like so many other aspects of car design, in the 1973 oil crisis. Consumers were becoming more and more concerned with the costs associated with running the family car and this had, in turn, led to the rise of models such as the Astra, Escort and Golf. These new, economical and convenient cars had taken over the family car market and the larger car suffered as a result. This was clearly evident when the Escort displaced the Cortina at the top of the bestseller charts. But there was still a call for the larger family car and most of the major manufacturers acted accordingly.

At the start of the 1980s British Leyland's Morris Marina was looking very dated when compared with the competition. This was the chance for British Leyland to step forward and change the fortunes of the ailing marque. But, in 1980, it chose to replace the Marina with the **Morris Ital**, a car that was already out of date before it was even launched. Again, British Leyland had failed to look to the future and instead sought refuge in the past. The Ital was not received at all well which is why it was the last car to ever wear a Morris badge. By 1984 the Ital had been replaced by the **Montego**, which it was hoped would be able to compete with the Ford Sierra and Vauxhall Cavalier.

The Ital was mediocre at best – at a time when rivals were producing much better cars.

The Montego was effectively a saloon version of the Maestro. In Turbo form it was quick but unruly.

The Montego was certainly an improvement on the Ital and offered a credible alternative to the smaller Maestro. The same S-Series engine that was introduced to the Maestro range powered the car and MG and Vanden Plas variants were also released, to add a bit of panache. Despite the improvements over the Ital, the Montego was not a huge success. It was finally discontinued in 1995 after selling less than half a million units in 15 years. The car suffered from the usual British Leyland problems of over-long development phases and dated engineering practices and it certainly didn't threaten the Cavalier, Cortina and Sierra.

The Ford Sierra was a bestseller largely thanks to massive corporate sales; company car drivers loved it.

When a Sierra saloon was introduced it was fitted with Sapphire badges to differentiate it from the regular hatch.

Of the mainstream car makers, nobody else offered an open-topped family car; the Vauxhall Cavalier had the sector to itself.

British Leyland was a very different company from Ford, with different philosophies and different global marketing strategies. While British Leyland was looking inwards, Ford was busy conquering the world and the vanguard of this conquest was the Escort. The success of the Escort showed that consumers were no longer so concerned about big cars. They wanted something roomy and stylish, but not large and ungainly, and the Escort fitted the bill perfectly. With the Escort and the Fiesta, Ford controlled the small family car and supermini markets, but it was not content and the Sierra was released to ensure that its domination over the competition would be complete.

When the public first saw the **Ford Sierra** it reacted with mixed emotions. Ford had decided to swap the harsh lines of the **Cortina** for the new, smoother Aeroback design, something that earned the Sierra the soubriquet 'the Jelly mould'. But Ford had thought ahead, looked at styling trends and built for the future. By the time the Sierra was ten years old it didn't look anywhere near as dated as its rivals and the facelift of 1987 made further improvements to the car. The Sierra was ahead of its time and as the public

The MkV was the last Ford to wear Cortina badges, before the Sierra replaced it in 1982.

While Ford and Vauxhall battled it out a German manufacturer was gaining popularity

caught up the car became more and more popular. The introduction of the Sapphire saloon was also a smart move by Ford; enticing consumers who preferred a saloon style to join the relentless march of Ford. By 1993 the Sierra's revolution was over and it was replaced by another successful car, the Mondeo. In its ten-year life the Sierra had sold 1.3 million units, achieving what Ford had set out to do and securing a position in the market for the forthcoming Mondeo.

LARGE FAMILY CARS OF THE 80S

1. Morris Ital
2. MG Montego
3. Ford Sierra
4. Vauxhall Cavalier
5. Ford Cortina
6. Audi 100

By the end of the 1980s Vauxhall had three cars in the top ten bestsellers of the decade; the Nova, Astra and Cavalier. They were becoming a serious threat to Ford, competing with them in all the major car classes. The **Vauxhall Cavalier** was a huge success, winning award after award as soon as it was released and it outsold the Sierra quite comfortably. By 1988 Vauxhall had begun selling the MkIII, a totally revamped car that abandoned the now dated look of the MkII Cavalier. The new style was more akin to the Sierra and although the Cavalier continued to outsell Ford's car, the new looks of the Cavalier helped the Sierra's sales figures, as it no longer looked so different from the competition. Even so, it would not be until 1994 that Ford finally managed to overtake the Cavalier in terms of sales, when the Mondeo finally broke its amazing run.

While Ford and Vauxhall battled it out a German manufacturer was quietly gaining popularity and making a name for itself in the larger car market. Ford had been beaten in the European Car of the Year award, in 1983, by the **Audi 100** and the car had been impressing consumers and critics right across Europe. It was aerodynamically efficient, making it not only economical to run, but also stylish and, of course, it benefitted from first-class German engineering. Audi had been around for many

In Avant (estate) form, the Audi 100 was a seriously stylish and practical load lugger.

years, but had never really been a big seller in the UK. The 100 was a statement of intent and Audi would soon become more prominent with the release of the A ranges. The Germans were becoming more and more powerful and during the 1990s they would experience even greater success.

With its 0.30 drag coefficient, the Audi 100 was far more aerodynamic than most of its contemporaries.

During the 1980s large family cars were not in such high demand and there was a dip in sales as consumers went for smaller models that were more convenient and economical to run. In addition, the spectre of the damage that cars were causing to the environment was beginning to raise its head, and this didn't bode well for the future of the large family car. After years of popularity the large car was beginning to wane. As the decade rolled on it saw the emergence of the SUV, which further threatened the existence of the larger car, and the future for this once default market segment was far from certain. Once again, the consumer had shaped the motor industry.

The Series 3 would be the last of the elegant Jaguar XJ models, before the arrival of the square-cut XJ40.

Luxury Cars

The luxury car market belonged to the Germans during the 1980s. Jaguar had success with the Series 3 XJ6, but it was BMW, Mercedes and Audi which led the way in terms of engineering excellence and quality. During the 1970s the Germans had stated their intent and during the 80s they would cement their position – but the British still had something to offer.

Jaguar had managed to hold off the advancing Germans during the preceding decade, with its XJS and XJ6, but it had made a mistake with the Series 2 XJ6. It had taken its eye off the ball and the Series 2 was plagued with reliability and build quality problems. However, the **Series 3 XJ6** was a huge improvement and it went on to be Jaguar's bestselling model, enabling it to compete with the Germans for a while longer. The three engine sizes – 3.4-litre straight-six, 4.2-litre straight-six and the 5.3-litre V12 – catered for all tastes and all but the smallest engine size now incorporated fuel injection systems. In 1984, the Sovereign badge was applied to the top of the range XJ6, further increasing the model's prestige. But the XJ6 was fighting a losing battle.

During the 1970s the Germans had started to make a name for themselves in the luxury car market and Jaguar's problems with the Series 2 XJ6 had come at just the wrong time. Mercedes had been working on the stunning **W124**, better known as the

Mercedes-Benz had been working on the stunning W124, better known as the E-Class

E-Class, during the early part of the decade and on its release, in 1985, it proved to be revolutionary. Undertrays beneath the car, along with the car's incredible drag co-efficient, meant that the new E-Class was

The W124 was an incredibly capable car, and no more so than when in Porsche-built 500E form, as here.

The W124 was beautifully built, aerodynamic and refined – plus it was spacious and powerful too. The perfect luxury car.

economical and very quiet. Sensors in the exhaust system ensured that the engine ran as efficiently as possible and even the single windscreen wiper would extend during motion to enable the entire windscreen to be cleaned. Mercedes' reputation for safety was further enhanced by the W124, as the car was able to withstand a 35mph crash into a concrete wall without major damage to the occupants. The dashboard was internally lined with aluminum to stop excessive penetration during a crash, airbags and height-adjustable seatbelts improved driver and passenger safety, and even the doors were designed to open easily after an impact.

The W124 effortlessly combined safety, reliability and luxury to produce one of the finest luxury cars ever built. Inside the E-Class were the required leather seats, thick carpets and wooden finishes. But there was also a Bose sound system and dual-zone automatic climate control. The steering wheel, seats and external mirrors were serviced with an electrical memory system, storing settings for up to three passengers.

'I have a BMW, but only because it stands for Bob Marley and the Wailers' Bob Marley

There was also a performance version of the W124, the 500E, which was powered by a monstrous 5-litre 32-valve V8 engine. The car was developed with the help of Porsche, another dominant German manufacturer.

The second-generation 5-Series, known as the E28, would be the first edition with an M5 option. The car has become a legend.

It's hard to believe now, but back in the 1980s **Audi** was only just beginning to really build a name for itself in the UK. Its cars were beautifully built and very well engineered, but they were always seen as a left-field choice, which is why its **100** and **200** never really sold in significant numbers. That certainly wasn't the case for **BMW** though, whose **5-Series** was already starting to become the default choice for anyone wanting a premium executive car; at this stage Ford, Vauxhall and Rover still had the lion's share of the market.

The BMW 7-Series has long offered discreet luxury performance. This is the second generation, known as the E32.

You could buy your 5-Series in saloon or estate bodystyles and if you wanted something seriously sporty but discreet, there was always the potent straight-six powered M5. But anyone wanting something particularly luxurious could opt for a **7-Series**, which like its smaller sibling was aimed at those wanting to do their own driving; it was amazingly good dynamically for something so large.

Of course, when it comes to luxury, the sky is the limit. The Germans may have been producing excellent, luxury cars for the mass market, but they were still a long way from the likes of Bentley and Rolls-Royce, when it came to uber-luxury. In 1985 Bentley revealed its **Turbo R**, a car that was designed to mix performance and opulence, in a large car.

The R in the name stood for 'road-holding', a major selling point for the Turbo R, and the car contained the 6.75-litre engine from the Mulsanne Turbo, with the addition of a fuel-injection system that produced around 300bhp. This excess of power would take the Turbo R to 60mph in under 7 seconds and allow it to reach a top speed of 143mph, which was impressive for a car that weighed two tons. Mainstream British carmakers may have been flagging by the 1980s, but Bentley still knew how to make a luxury car. The inside of the Turbo R featured luxurious leather seats, walnut surrounds on the doors, lambswool carpets, heated seats, and climate control. It was a cut above the rest and sold well, with more than 7,000 units being produced between 1985 and 1997.

A sister car to the Turbo R was the **Rolls-Royce Silver Spirit**, which was released in 1980 and was the first Rolls to feature the retractable Spirit of Ecstasy mascot in the radiator surround. The Silver Spirit may have shared the floorplan with the older Silver Shadow, but it utilised new shock absorbers and self-levelling suspension to improve on its predecessor. The Silver Spirit led to several later versions and was produced by Rolls-Royce until 1998.

> 'At 60mph the loudest noise in the Rolls-Royce comes from the electric clock' David Ogilvy

During the 1980s the British were still the kings of super luxury. No one could quite manage the aristocratic levels of refinery that Rolls-Royce and Bentley could, but these cars were really evolutionary and not revolutionary. The Germans were slowly improving in the luxury car market and it wouldn't be long before they were able to combine the reliability, power and heritage of German car engineering with the luxury the British upper class demanded. The 1980s was a time of great wealth generation and many people, especially in the City of London, were getting very rich, very quickly. This

The Turbo R was an evolution of the Bentley Mulsanne, which had started out as the Rolls-Royce Silver Spirit.

For those wanting more, there were plenty of companies happy to turn a Silver Spirit into something more spacious, opulent and costly.

new money was increasing the demand for high-end luxury cars and over the following decades this section of the car market would become more competitive. As the 1980s drew to a close it was too close to call between the British and the Germans as to who would control the luxury market during the 1990s.

The Silver Spirit superseded the Silver Shadow, but underneath there were many parts carried over.

LUXURY CARS OF THE 80S

1. Jaguar Series 3 XJ6
2. Mercedes E-Class W124
3. Audi 100 and 200
4. BMW 5-Series
5. BMW 7-Series
6. Bentley Turbo R
7. Rolls-Royce Silver Spirit

The Alfa Romeo Spider had first appeared in the 1960s, and would last right the way through to the 1990s.

Sports Cars

The 1980s is often seen as a decade of excess, despite its origins in recession and social and political strife. The sports car was, to some degree, destined to spend the next ten years rediscovering its roots. By the start of the 1980s the traditional sports roadster had largely been usurped. Cars such as the 911 Turbo and Jaguar's XJ models had delivered comfort and safety with barely a performance penalty. The original idea of sports cars as convertibles would be revived during the 1980s and the decade was to produce some noteworthy classics, such as the third-generation **Mercedes SL**, the revised **Alfa Romeo Spider**, **Mazda MX-5** and the **Lotus Elan**. It would also herald the age of the true supercar, in the form of the Ferrari F40, and Porsche 959, both capable of around 200mph. Along with these desirable, high-end cars there would also be a continuation in the

The 1980s would be the decade of roadsters and record breakers. Ferrari and Porsche would battle it out to break the 200mph barrier and the Japanese would compete to be named the king of the roadster. These car wars would culminate in some of the finest and most successful sports cars ever made.

development of very fast production road cars such as the powerful Ford Sierra Cosworth and the Renault 5 Turbo. Speed and performance were back, and the 1980s delivered them in spades.

In 1983, The Frankfurt Motor Show saw the first incarnation of a true supercar – the **Porsche 959**. The 959, known at first as the Gruppe B, was produced for the Group B racing series, the rules of which stipulated

Later versions of the Alfa Romeo Spider, as shown here, were available with left-hand drive only.

that at least 200 road-legal versions of each competing car had to be produced. Although later the Group B series was scrapped, due to a series of horrific accidents, the die had been cast and the supercar had arrived on the public road. The 959 was a truly innovative car. It may have built on the success of the 911 but there were many differences. The majority of the bodywork was constructed from Kevlar, while the doors and bootlid were made of lightweight aluminium. There was a redeveloped front end and a distinctive spoiler, which enabled the car to hug the ground at high speeds. One of the biggest differences between the 959 and the standard 911 was that the 959 was four-wheel drive. An innovative, computer-controlled clutch (known as the Porsche-Steur Kuppling) split the torque evenly between the front and rear ends in treacherous conditions, or guaranteed 80 per cent of the power to the rear wheels under intense acceleration.

When the roadgoing version of the 959 was officially released in April 1987, its price tag was £150,000 – three times the cost of the 911 – but this didn't stop Porsche producing just short of 300 units in 14 months. The official statistics were even more mind-boggling. It produced 443bhp and had a top speed of 197mph, making it officially the fastest production car in the world.

'If one does not fail at times, then one has not challenged himself'

Ferdinand Porsche

Impressive as the Porsche 959 undoubtedly was, its reign as the king of speed didn't last long. The young pretender to the throne was **Ferrari's F40**, regarded by many as the greatest supercar ever made. The F40 was conceived to mark the anniversary of Enzo Ferrari's 40 years in the business. Since

The Porsche 959 was a technological tour de force, with massive power, four-wheel drive, and a high-tech bodyshell construction.

The Ford Sierra RS Cosworth was a landmark car of the 1980s, with that massive rear wing becoming iconic on its own.

producing his first car in 1947, the 125S, Enzo Ferrari had consistently designed some of the finest cars on the planet and the F40 was no different. It was a no-frills speed machine. Constructed from Kevlar and glass fibre, to save weight, the F40 had Ferrari's long racing heritage to thank for its extraordinary abilities. The F40 was capable of going from 0–60 in just 4.7 seconds and with a top speed of 201mph it topped the 959 as the world's fastest production car.

The F40 was a truly groundbreaking car. It broke the 200mph limit for the first time (for a road car) and was created as a direct result of Ferrari's Formula 1 research and development programme. The F40 officially went into production in 1988 and over the next four years it trebled its original estimate, achieving 1,311 units sold, an impressive feat when it's considered that the UK price tag was a hefty £193,299.

Despite the fact that the F40 and 959 are now more than 20 years old, they are still two of the finest road cars ever made. They represent an era when speed was more important then safety and environmental concerns, and they would both give today's supercars a run for their money. However, while these cars could achieve speeds that even now are far from commonplace, the newer breed of supercars are more usable and efficient than anything from the 1980s.

While Ferrari and Porsche were vying for the title of the fastest car in the world, more prolific manufacturers were also breaking out of the restrictions of the 1970s. In 1986, Ford unveiled its **Sierra RS Cosworth** to great acclaim. The Sierra was the replacement for the ageing Cortina, but the RS Cosworth appeared light years away from that classic car. This was a true monster of the road. The poor man's supercar it might have been, but it was capable of 0–60 in a time that was just over a second slower than the F40. With a top

The Ferrari F40 was the first production road car to break the 200mph barrier; they're now hugely sought after.

The mid-engined Renault 5 Turbo 2 was absolutely insane, and made a great racing machine.

SPORTS CARS OF THE 80S

1. Mercedes SL
2. Alfa Romeo Spider
3. Mazda MX-5
4. Lotus Elan
5. Porsche 959
6. Ferrari F40
7. Ford Sierra Cosworth
8. Renault 5 Turbo
9. MG Metro 6R4
10. Toyota MR2

speed of 145mph the RS Cosworth ushered in an era of fast street cars that were accessible to the average person. The RS Cosworth shared the 1980s with other notable street racers such as the **Renault 5 Turbo**, capable of 124mph, which won the Monte Carlo rally in 1984 and the insane **MG Metro 6R4**, which, like the 959, was created for the Group B racing series. This monster version of the little car, so commonplace on the high streets of Britain, was fitted with a V6 3-litre engine that produced some 250bhp. It had a top speed of only 110mph, but was capable of achieving 0–60 quicker than the 959 or the F40!

'If you buy the engine, I will give you everything else for free' Enzo Ferrari

The 1980s was notable for another type of sports car – the roadster. In the sports car world the roadster had fallen out of favour. Convertible, two-seater sports cars were not as popular as the GTs, the racing behemoths of Ferrari and Porsche, or the beefed-up production cars of Ford or Renault, but the 1980s saw the 'traditional' sports car make a resurgence. **Toyota's MR2**, Lotus' Elan and Mazda's MX-5 all made serious impacts on the market, but it was Mazda that perhaps had the most success.

The Mazda MX-5, or Miata as it was known in the US, was released in 1989 and became an instant classic. It was a well made and well designed car that harked back to the original roadster concept. Capable of 115mph, the little car was more than enough to satisfy the mass market, and the price tag of under £8,000 made it more than affordable. The MX-5 led the way in the rebirth of the two-seater roadster and over the next two decades many manufacturers attempted to copy it. But, to date, the MX-5 is still the most popular two-seater sports car in the world.

The 1980s produced some of the finest sports cars in history. The shackles of the 70s were thrown off, leading to developments in all categories of racing cars. The Group B racing series may have died young, but it enabled a new mindset in sports car design that was to set the foundations for the next 20 years. Sports cars were to get faster and super-fast versions of standard production cars were to become the norm. Speed was back, and cars were only going to get quicker.

The Toyota MR2 marked a return of the affordable sports car.

Most SUV fans reckon the Range Rover is the original and best of the luxury 4x4s.

SUVs

With the release of the Range Rover, Land Rover had given birth to a new vehicle class – the luxury Sports Utility Vehicle, or SUV. The SUV would challenge the large family car during the decades to come and it would also get more and more luxurious. But during the 1980s the SUV was still in its infancy.

Up to the release of the **Range Rover**, in 1970, the 4x4 was very much seen as a utility vehicle. It was the 'car' of choice for farmers, American ranchers and those involved in rugged, outdoor work. The 4x4 was simply a tool that helped farmers traverse their fields, or explorers get through the Amazon, or across the plains of Africa. They were sparse, functional, loud, noisy and uncomfortable and certainly not something to be seen driving around London in. But within the space of two decades this had all changed. The 4x4 had become the SUV; rugged and loud had become comfortable and quiet; and the 4x4 had become a status symbol to some, and the scourge of the road to others.

This automotive revolution was started by Land Rover during the 1970s, but the Range Rover wasn't meant to be a new type of vehicle. It was meant to compete in the American market with existing 4x4s from the likes of Jeep, and the early Range Rovers were very utilitarian by today's standards. They were designed to be rugged and hard-wearing. The seats were vinyl, the interior was made predominantly of plastic and was built so that it could be easily cleaned.

Under the bonnet, the engines went through numerous changes and replacements as the Range Rover carved out its niche.

The 4x4 had become the SUV; rugged and loud had become quiet and comfortable

At first the Range Rover came in two-door form only, but in time there would be a four-door offering as well.

In 1984, the engine was fitted with a Lucas fuel injection system, disposing of the now outdated carburettor technology and boosting the power output to 155bhp. The 3.5-litre engine was increased to 3.9 litres by the end of the decade and in the early 1990s a 4.2-litre variant was introduced. It was important that the Range Rover also had a diesel variant and after a long development phase, code-named 'Project Beaver', a 2.4-litre turbo-diesel, delivering a lacklustre 112bhp, was added to the burgeoning engine range. The diesel project had provided a great deal of experience and knowledge for the engineers

When it comes to SUVs, the Land Rover brand still carries more cachet than any other, despite often woeful reliability.

at Land Rover and it would help them further develop the 4x4 as the years unfolded. During the project several world records were broken, such as the first SUV to reach 100mph, the furthest a SUV had managed to go in 24 hours and a host of other achievements.

In 1984 a four-door version of the Range Rover became available. This was an important step as it changed the utility vehicle into one that had real potential for everyday, family use. The groundwork had been set and when Land Rover released the next generation Range Rover, in 1994, it would be aimed at a different market.

Land Rover had real heritage when it came to 4x4s. The **Land Rover One Ten** had begun production in 1983 and it was unbeatable as a hard-working 4x4. Powerful engines and premium build quality all ensured that no self-respecting adventurer would set out into the unknown without one, and this provenance would serve Land Rover well when it decided to offer a version of the One Ten as a private vehicle. Branded as the County, the Land Rover made the jump from working 4x4 to family SUV. Differing paint jobs, the

The County was Land Rover's attempt at making its classic model a bit more civilised for family use.

If anybody can claim to have beaten Land Rover at its own game, it's Jeep, which started building 4x4s in the 1940s.

When Land Rover released the next generation Range Rover it would be aimed at a different market

addition of radio-cassette players and other luxuries enticed the public to buy the car. In late 1990 the One Ten became known as the Defender and firmly established itself in the family car market.

In terms of worldwide competition, Land Rover had some fairly capable adversaries during the 1980s. Jeep was a major American car manufacturer which had already seen the potential of the 4x4 as a family car. With America's wide-open spaces and rural landscape, the SUV had already become a popular car for families right across the country. The **XJ Cherokee** was first introduced in 1984 and it utilised the monocoque design that had been embraced by Land Rover in its Range Rover. During 1984, in the United States, Jeep revealed the Wagoneer, which could seriously challenge the popular station wagon. The **XJ Wagoneer** was available in a 'Limited' version which had leather seats and wood trim, making the car much more amenable to families looking for an alternative vehicle to the norm. The Wagoneer wasn't available in the UK until 1983, but when it began to be seen in this country it showed what the new SUV could offer. Jeep kept pushing the boundaries of the SUV

Jeeps were perfectly suited to the big open spaces of the US, but were too large for European buyers.

by offering a two-wheel drive version of the Cherokee, in 1985, which further removed the SUV from its traditional 4x4 roots.

Toyota was also in the market and its **70 Series Land Cruiser** first came to prominence during 1984. Initially just a short-wheelbase version was available, but this would develop through the following decade. Toyota had an excellent track record in making utility vehicles and its **Hilux** had led the way since the 1970s. Today, it's one of the most common 4x4s in the world and the technology used for the Hilux was adapted for use in the Land Cruiser.

The rough and ready nature of the 4x4 wouldn't last long. These workhorses were now called SUVs, lending them a softer image. The SUV was a car that could carry a definite image. It could be marketed at people who liked the great outdoors, offering an added

SUVS OF THE 80S

1. Range Rover
2. Land Rover One Ten
3. Jeep XJ Cherokee
4. Jeep XJ Wagoneer
5. Toyota 70 Series Land Cruiser
6. Toyota Hilux

The Toyota Land Cruiser has long been one of the most capable 4x4s when it comes to off roading.

'I'd rather have a Range Rover than a $40,000 painting'

Chris Evert

value to the traditional family car. Safety was another good selling point as the SUV was a big vehicle, built to survive the elements, so owners could be confident that in an accident they would be safe. However, despite these plus points, the SUV was a controversial car. They were hardly fuel-efficient and although they were undoubtedly safe for the occupants, anything that they hit was not going to come off so lightly. They were also difficult to park and most people who owned one, as a family car, were not really driving it across the wild and windy plains, particularly in Britain.

By the end of the 1990s the SUV would have largely overcome these issues and it would become a fixture in the range of most large manufacturers, an impressive feat for a vehicle class that really only happened by chance.

By mixing capability with astonishing reliability, Toyota usurped Land Rover's position in many global markets.

1990s

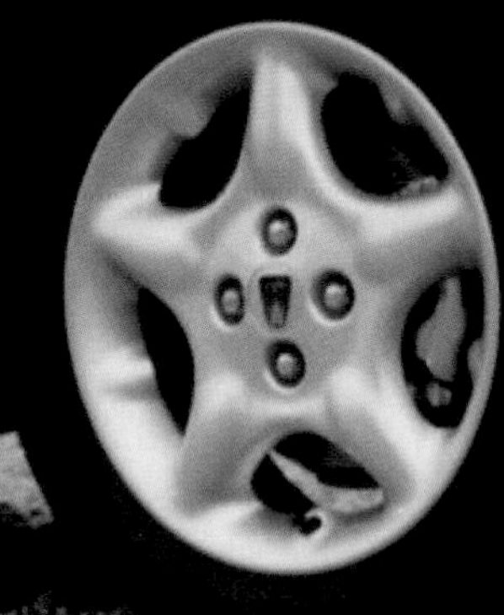

10 Bestsellers

As we have seen, in the 1980s in particular, the young and upwardly mobile craved sporty cars, but for those who couldn't afford the hefty price tag, there were many other ways that the dream could be obtained; loud exhausts, racing stripes and big wheels all allowed the ordinary to become unique. But, by the middle of the 1990s, things were changing again.

When, in 1997, New Labour came to power it finally signalled the end of the 1980s excess and flamboyance. The 1990s was to be a decade of muted advances, rather than technological leaps. The country had tired of YUPPIE culture and there was a collective yearning for a return to traditional values. Manufacturers were quick to exploit the new trends in society.

The 1990s saw average road speeds reduced. That isn't to say that cars became slower or less desirable – they didn't. The average speed that ordinary cars were capable of continued to rise and high-end manufacturers produced some extraordinary cars, which remained the apple of many people's eye. But mainstream carmakers began to emphasise things such as safety and economy over speed. The racing lines of Ford's XR3i and Sierra were replaced with the more staid Focus and Mondeo. Volkswagen turned its back on powerful cars such as the Corrado and released a reincarnation of the Beetle. Toyota followed suit with its first hybrid car; the Prius, and the French manufacturer, Renault, introduced the award winning Scenic; the compact people-carrier had arrived and it was to become the distinctive car of the 1990s.

of the 1990s

1.

• STATS AND FACTS •

HAIL TO THE KING
The Fiesta dominated the 1990s and was the most popular new car in Britain in 1990, 1991, 1996, 1997 and 1998. It is still popular today.

CHANGING TRENDS
In the first 12 years of its life almost 1.3 million units had been sold in Britain and things continued to get better – an impressive feat for a small car.

It seemed that Ford could do no wrong with the Fiesta; buyers just lapped them up. This is a MkIV edition.

Ford Fiesta

The Fiesta showed its potential during the 1980s as a small car that could take on its bigger rivals. By the start of the 1990s the little car had become one of the most popular models on the road and its dominance would continue through to the end of the decade. This was just as well for Ford, as the elevated position the company had enjoyed in the market during the 1980s would be severely tested in the 1990s.

The MkIII Fiesta went on sale at the beginning of 1989 and despite the fact that it had many similarities with its predecessors internally, on the outside it was a radical departure from the MkII. A five-door model was added to the range and the Fiesta now looked softer in shape. The 1.8-litre version was so successful that it sold one million units in its first two years of production. The XR2 model was also updated, with a 16v Zetec engine, although in 1994 the XR2i badge was dropped and the legendary racer was no more. The badge had become too synonymous with boy racers and although a sporty Fiesta was still available, the Si, it wasn't quite the same. Nevertheless, Ford now knew that it was onto a winner and, after steadily improving the standard MkIII with refinements, such as fuel-injected engines, it soon released the MkIV.

Arriving in 1995, the MkIV carried on the Fiesta's success, but it was a far different car to its forebears. The Fiesta not only looked different but also had a completely overhauled suspension system and a new Zetec engine. In 1999 a facelift was applied to the UK's now bestselling car. The new version of the MkIV was mainly a cosmetic update, and that was all it had to be. Ford stuck to its usual mantra of not messing with a winning formula and the Fiesta continued its dominace in the UK. During the 1990s plenty of companies produced cars to emulate the Fiesta, but none of them were really in its league.

Ford now knew it was onto a winner

Small no longer meant basic, as the Fiesta could be ordered with a reasonably opulent specification. This is a MkIII.

2. Ford Escort

At the start of the 1990s Ford was the biggest player in the UK car market, and at the end of the decade it had the two most popular cars on the road; the Fiesta and the Escort. It was a sign of the times. The days of the big Cortina were gone and even the mighty Escort had been supplanted by the diminutive Fiesta. Despite the UK's preference for smaller cars, the Escort held firm in the medium-size car market. But now it would have Vauxhall hard on its heels with the Vectra, Cavalier and Astra.

The MkV Escort was in the showrooms for the end of 1990, but it didn't have the impact that Ford was hoping for. The car looked reasonably different, but the press and public weren't impressed. The build quality was below par, with reports of premature corrosion, and the fact that the car didn't handle that well gave the MkV a rather inauspicious start.

• STATS AND FACTS •

BESTSELLER

By the 1990s, the Ford Escort was the bestselling car of all time in the UK, selling more than four million units in Britain alone.

MKIII BECOMES THE BEST

The Escort had been popular for years, but the MkIII version would prove to be the most popular version of all, allowing it to continue gracing Ford's forecourts.

Undeterred, Ford released a revised MkV in 1992 and kept on improving, in a bid to give the car's image a boost. The introduction of 16v Zetec engines helped, as did the return of the XR3i version. Slowly but surely the Escort was clinging on. The MkVI, released in 1995, continued the modifications.

The Escort MkV was a missed opportunity for Ford; it only sold in big numbers because of the company's marketing might.

The third-generation Astra was a heavily revised version of its predecessor. Vauxhall offered it in hatchback, estate or convertible forms.

3. Vauxhall Astra

After its promising start, the Astra continued to impress. In 1991 Vauxhall introduced the MkIII Astra, which built on the MkII, without really setting the world alight. Even so, the MkIII was one of the first cars on the road to start taking safety seriously. It was fitted with twin side-impact bars, airbags and a toughened safety cage. The top of the range GSi models were also impressive, and not just in terms of safety. They sported a 2-litre 16v engine that delivered a more than adequate 150bhp, but it was short-lived as increasing insurance costs saw it discontinued in 1994.

The Astra sold well enough not to require a replacement until 1998, when the new MkIV version took the car through to the new millennium and continued the evolution of this plucky little survivor. The Astra had dared to challenge the superiority of the Escort and had not disgraced itself. Vauxhall was now becoming a serious threat to Ford and the Astra helped Vauxhall to stay in the market and further challenge Ford's dominance of the medium car sector.

• STATS AND FACTS •

BABY FACE

Vauxhall's European television commercial for the Astra showed a baby lecturing thousands of other babies on the merits of the car.

DOUBLE VISION

In South Africa, the Astra won the title of 'Car of the Year' in two consecutive years in 1992 and 1993, which was strange as it was the same car.

4. Ford Mondeo

Ford launched the replacement for the Sierra in 1993. It was a major undertaking and Ford invested over $5.5 billion in its development. The truth is that Ford had little choice. Its cars were gaining a reputation for shoddiness and cost cutting. With Vauxhall improving, the Mondeo had to be a seriously good car. Despite its flaws, it was a success and spawned a second generation, in 1996. The MkII looked appealing and refined the MkI, setting the foundations for a very successful car.

• STATS AND FACTS •

WORLDWIDE IMPACT
The name of Ford's successor to the Sierra is derived from the Latin word 'mundus', which means world.

INTERNATIONAL PRESENCE
The Mondeo was sold in America, Brazil, Mexico and across Asia – as well as throughout Europe. It's predominantly manufactured in Belgium.

5. Vauxhall Cavalier

In the early 1990s Vauxhall showed its mettle as the Cavalier began to outsell the Sierra. Ford was on the ropes and the Cavalier went from strength to strength, even against the new Mondeo. By 1990 the Cavalier was on its third mark and was still going strong. This final version was the best, showing improvements in all areas. The MkIII also gave a nod to its heritage with the release of the 200bhp Cavalier Turbo. Vauxhall would next build on the Cavalier with the release of the Vectra.

• STATS AND FACTS •

GHOSTS OF THE PAST
When the MkIII Cavalier was released the Vectra name was not adopted, as Vauxhall feared drawing parallels with the much-maligned Vauxhall Victor.

SECOND PLACE
The Cavalier's best year for sales was 1992, when it was the second bestselling car in Britain, behind the Ford Escort.

6. Rover 200

The Rover 200 replaced the Triumph Acclaim that resulted from the Rover/Honda alliance. The 200 was intended as an upmarket four-door saloon, powered by a 1.3-litre Honda engine, or the more powerful 1.6-litre British Leyland version. It sold well and the mid-90s saw a major refit. The new car was smaller and completely redesigned, but it was not aimed at competing with the Fiesta and Corsa, but rather the Astra and Escort, which it was never really capable of doing.

• STATS AND FACTS •

JAPANESE INSPIRATION
The first generation of the Rover 200 was a four-door saloon based on the Honda Ballade.

CHINESE TAKEAWAY
Production rights and tooling for the Rover 200, but not the name, now belong to the Chinese firm, Nanjing Automotive.

The Mondeo was a huge improvement over the outdated Sierra.

The Cavalier was a good car, but never managed to outsell Ford's offerings.

The 200 was neatly designed, especially in Turbo Coupé form as here.

It was the UK's first Corsa, but Europe's second edition.

7. Vauxhall Corsa

The first UK edition of the Corsa was introduced to the market in 1993. Vauxhall finally dropped the Nova badge and the new car was aimed squarely at taking the Fiesta's throne. The new Corsa brought a European style to the boxy Nova. It was viewed as more of a small family car, as opposed to the 'teenager's car' that it had been before, and accordingly the SR versions were dropped. The car was a success but didn't really have the handling and ride of others in its class. It was marketed in 1.2, 1.4 and 1.6-litre varieties, along with a nippy 1.5-litre diesel variant, which catered for all tastes.

• STATS AND FACTS •

SLOW STARTER
The Vauxhall Corsa only became available in the UK market in 1993. But, in the rest of the world, it had been available since 1982.

HORSES FOR COURSES
Released in 1993, the Corsa B offered no saloon version, except in the Latin American market, where saloons are preferable to hatchbacks.

The Vectra replaced the Cavalier, but the Mondeo was better.

8. Vauxhall Vectra

Appearing in 1988, the Vectra was the model chosen by Vauxhall to replace the successful Cavalier. The Vectra substituted a smoother appearance for the Cavalier's dated lines and the car was a serious threat to the Mondeo. An updated model arrived in 1992, which refreshed the Vectra to keep it in line with its peers. In 1995 the Vectra B continued the car's evolution, but had the distinction of being the final model to be produced at the company's Luton factory. The Vectra remained in Vauxhall's line-up for years and was a favourite for hire-car companies due to its build quality and reliability.

• STATS AND FACTS •

NOT TO ALL TASTES
Top Gear's Jeremy Clarkson stated the Vectra was 'designed in a coffee break by people who couldn't care less about cars'.

ESTATES ON ESTATES
The most rare Vectras are the estate GSi models, with only 317 ever having been produced.

The facelifted Metro would ultimately become the Rover 100.

9. Rover MG Metro

By the 1990s the Metro had been on the road for quite some time. The rise of the Fiesta and Corsa had severely hindered it, but nevertheless, thanks to a new Rover badge, and excellent build quality the Metro was voted the *What Car?* Supermini Car of the Year, in 1991. It is a measure of how well the Metro did that it made the top ten cars of the decade at all. In 1994 Rover scrapped the name, choosing Rover 100 instead. In truth the Metro had probably outlived its purpose. The future belonged not to British companies, but foreign manufacturers with new ideas, designs and working practices.

• STATS AND FACTS •

FALSE HOPE
The Metro sold over one million units in the UK during its lifespan, but it didn't help the fortunes of British car manufacturers.

NAME CHANGE
In 1994, Rover changed the name of the car to the Rover 100 and it continued to sell well, despite its outdated technology.

The most practical Sierra of all was the estate edition.

10. Ford Sierra

Like the Metro, by the start of the 1990s the Sierra was a dying breed. The car had served Ford well as a stopgap between the resilient Cortina and the future Mondeo, and this is reflected in its status at the bottom of the top ten cars of the 1990s. Despite the Sierra's problems it still sold incredibly well. It holds the distinction of being the 10th most sold car in UK motoring history, with some 1.3 million units being sold throughout its production life. It will be fondly remembered for transporting British families around the country in comfort and tearing up racetracks in its various Cosworth forms.

• STATS AND FACTS •

GLOBE TROTTER
The Sierra was a truly international car, being produced in Germany, Belgium, the UK, Argentina, Venezuela, South Africa and New Zealand.

PROJECT TONI
The code name for the Sierra during its production phase was 'Project Toni'. Thankfully the name didn't stick.

In RS Turbo form, the Fiesta MkIII was one of the hottest hatches available.

Minis and Superminis

The 1990s was the first decade in which the small car became the preferred choice for the consumer. It was a trend that had been coming since the Escort had surpassed the larger Cortina, during the 1980s, and it was a natural evolution for the mass-market car.

During the 1990s, the **Ford Fiesta** was the bestselling car. For more than 20 years, Ford had owned the top spot; first with the Cortina, then the Escort and now the Fiesta, highlighting how small had become beautiful in the car market. The roots of this trend lay in the 1970s, when the world had become aware of its reliance on fossil fuels, which were steadily running

The more economical version of the MkIII Fiesta.

The original Clio proved to be a big hit for Renault.

out, and thereby becoming more expensive. This influenced public opinion, as well as the designs and future strategies of the carmakers, and over the course of the decade this revolution would continue.

The first true supermini to emerge during the 1990s was the **Renault Clio**, which was introduced to the public at the 1990 Paris Motor Show. Sales of Renault's world-beater began in the UK during the following year and it was an immediate hit with the British public. Renault had already had success in the sector with its 5, but the Clio was a vast improvement. It was bigger, which meant it was roomier for the occupants, which in turn made it a viable alternative to the traditional family car. As the car was small, so too could be its powerplant. Renault released the car with the choice of either a 1.2 or 1.4-litre engine, all of which were fuel injected after 1992 and enabled outstanding economy for

From Papa and Nicole, to Va va voom and Thierry Henry

The Nicole/Papa advertising campaign for the Clio would prove to be a massive success for Renault.

The Clio Williams would quickly become one of the most sought after hot hatches of the 1990s.

a family car. With everything the Clio had going for it, it wasn't surprising that it won the coveted European Car of the Year award, in 1991.

Over the course of the 1990s the first-generation Clio received a number of updates that further improved on the design and usability of the car. These updates were largely cosmetic, but in 1998 the Clio II was born, which brought with it a completely new look. The market responded kindly to the new, curvy supermini and it sold in huge numbers. The inside of the car was further refined from the Clio I, providing added comfort, which further appealed to the family sector. More plastic was utilised in the car's design, which meant that the car was less susceptible to rust and the engine range was updated to improve on economy. To capture the public's attention Renault embarked on an advertising campaign that became a classic. The campaign followed the lives of 'Nicole' and her 'papa' and featured the constant comical exchanges of 'Papa', 'Nicole', 'Papa', 'Nicole'. The advert placed the car firmly in the mind of the consumer and the country followed Nicole's quest for a husband, which culminated in a spoof of *The Graduate* when Nicole's husband was finally revealed. To everyone's surprise it turned out to be Vic Reeves, who was promptly jilted by Nicole, in favour of Bob Mortimer and his new Generation Clio. To give some idea of the campaign's success, it is estimated that over 23 million people watched the 'Vic and Bob' advert. The Clio had revolutionised the supermini market and the car was firmly placed within the popular culture of the 1990s.

The market responded kindly to the curvy new supermini

There was always a danger that the supermini could be seen as a car for women, something that would seriously inhibit its success as the 'new' family car. Renault was careful to balance the Papa/Nicole adverts with a manly, sport version of the Clio, ensuring its universal appeal. To celebrate its involvement with the Williams Formula 1 team, Renault released a special **Clio Williams**, in 1993, and it was a very smart move that was to spawn two further versions. The car had a 2-litre 16 valve engine that produced 150bhp. It also looked the part, decked out with gold trim, gold wheels and advanced brakes and suspension. Originally, Renault intended to make 3,800 of these super-Clios,

The Vauxhall Corsa carried on where the Nova left off.

but the car's popularity led to a further 1,500 being made and to this day it is still regarded as the best hot supermini ever created, bar none.

The Clio was a worthy competitor to the Fiesta, which went from strength to strength during the 1990s, and it encouraged other manufacturers to take on Ford's mini superstar. A possible suitor emerged in 1993 when Vauxhall unveiled the new **Corsa**. The Corsa B was the first version of Vauxhall's supermini to adopt the Corsa badge for the UK market. It was a simple and practical car that offered value for money and an economical and reliable alternative to the Clio and Fiesta. The Corsa sold well and easily made the top ten bestsellers in the country over the course of the decade. However, the car was fairly unremarkable. It did what it did well, but it couldn't really rival its competitors

The Corsa was the perfect city car, and was especially popular with women drivers.

The SEAT Ibiza shared its underpinnings with the Volkswagen Polo.

SEAT was launched as the sporty arm of the Volkswagen Group, but many of its models weren't that sporty.

in terms of fun, driving ability and style and this led to the car being completely revamped in 2000.

Two other notable superminis to emerge during the 1990s were the **SEAT Ibiza** and the **Volkswagen Polo**. The two companies shared much of the development of the two cars, as the Volkswagen Group owned SEAT. Consequently, the 1994 MkIII Polo shared many of its internal components with the Ibiza MkII, although outwardly they were very different. Volkswagen had already had success with its larger Golf and a smaller version was a logical alternative. The Polo received a facelift at the end of the decade, which guided it into the new century and the only thing that stopped it selling in greater numbers was its relatively expensive price tag. SEAT, too, had been producing its Ibiza since the mid-1980s and during the 1990s it would be further developed for the UK market.

The MkIII VW Polo was practical, fashionable and great to drive. Seen here is the 1995 CL.

Two other notable superminis to emerge during the 90s were the SEAT Ibiza and Volkswagen Polo

By the end of the decade the supermini was becoming a firm favourite with the British public. The small car had come on in leaps and bounds and by the end of the 2000s the supermini would account for a sizeable percentage of the top ten bestselling cars in the UK. Ford had led the charge of the supermini, but Renault had captured the imagination of the public through clever advertising, marketing and special edition versions of its Clio. The supermini had finally arrived, and it was here to stay.

SUPERMINIS OF THE 90S

1. Ford Fiesta
2. Renault Clio
3. Clio Williams
4. Vauxhall Corsa
5. SEAT Ibiza
6. Volkswagen Polo

By the mid-1990s the Escort was past its sell-by date, but lots of marketing kept it in the top ten.

Small Family Cars

The 1990s may have seen the rise of the supermini, but it also saw the small family car increase its influence in the UK market. Once again, Ford would lead the way, but the decade would also see Citroen and Peugeot increase in stature, and challenge the Astra and the Escort for supremacy.

In RS Cosworth form, the Ford Escort would become a genuine road rocket.

Small cars were now controlling the market and for those who had yet to be bitten by the supermini bug, there were plenty of alternatives in the small family car sector. By 1990, the venerable Escort, in one form or another, had been hovering around the bestseller list for over 20 years. It was going to have to be replaced with a new model, but this would not emerge until the end of the decade. In the meantime Ford would update the Escort three times during the decade, starting, in 1990, with the MkV.

By 1990, the MkIV Escort was beginning to show its age. It had been introduced during 1986 and as a result it still had the boxy looks of the previous decade. The **Escort MkV** embraced the curvy style that the Sierra had been far-sighted enough to embody years before. Like the Sierra, initially, the MkV Escort was not that well received. It was labelled 'uninspiring' and 'disappointing'

By 1990, the Escort had been hovering around the bestseller list for over 20 years

and the car suffered from reports of early corrosion and bad workmanship. This was something that Ford could not afford to be tarnished with and within two years it had given the MkV a facelift in an effort to alleviate the problems. The Escort MkVb revised the front grille, the rear end and incorporated the new Zetec engines in its design, all of which proved to be big improvements over the early model. By

The Escort sold well because of marketing; its replacement, the Focus, sold well because it was a truly great car.

In 1995, the Escort received its final makeover, when the MkVI was unveiled

1994, there were five trim levels available that ranged from the basic L to the Ghia Si, but there was also still a sports version in the form of the classic **Escort RS Cosworth**.

The RS Cosworth had been launched in 1992 and was the intended replacement for the Sapphire RS Cosworth. The Escort version used the turbocharged 2-litre 16-valve engine, was four-wheel drive and sported an enormous rear spoiler. The road-going version that, as usual, had been produced for homologation purposes, featured a smaller turbo than the racing version, but this didn't dim the public's desire for it. The original, and required, batch of 2,500 were sold in no time and Ford kept on building the car until 1996.

In 1995, the Escort received its final makeover, when the MkVI was unveiled. The underlying mechanics and bodywork of the car were the same as the previous iteration, but cosmetically it was completely revamped. The ride and handling were readily improved and the MkVI was also released in a rare GTi

Spacious, refined, well-equipped and fabulous to drive, the Focus was an instant hit.

The Astra convertible was designed to take on drop-top editions of the Ford Escort and Volkswagen Golf.

format. This occurred in 1997 and it was the only time that a Ford has featured a GTi badge. The GTi was something of a swansong for the Escort as it was replaced, in 1998, by the all-new **Ford Focus**.

The Focus really came to prominence during the 2000s, but it is an example of how far the small car had come during the preceding 20 years. It was a completely redesigned small family car and one that would prove to be a roaring success.

Ford was by no means the only manufacturer concentrating on the small family car during the 1990s. Vauxhall released two versions of its Astra during the decade with varying degrees of success. The **MkIII Astra**, released in 1991, sought to build on the reputation of the previous generation and offered new styling and the inclusion of safety features that were usually more associated with more expensive models. Twin side impact bars, a reinforced safety cage and a collapsible steering column all put the Astra ahead of its competitors in terms of safety and enabled Vauxhall to compete with the Escort for market share. However, the MkIII was, in other areas, somewhat of a disappointment. The suspension had a reputation for being soggy and the engineering was not exactly inspiring. If Vauxhall was serious about longevity then it needed an improved model. That came in 1998 with the **Astra MkIV**, which addressed many of the MkIII's problems. It received an excellent Euro NCAP rating of four stars and the new Ecotec engines helped to bring the Astra more in line with its peers.

This was just as well for Vauxhall as competition in the small family car sector was increasing all the time. 1991 saw the release

The ZX was launched into a segment that Citroen had vacated several years earlier; it was good value, but very cheaply made.

of the **Citroen ZX**, which was well received. Citroen had not produced a small family car for quite some time and had instead pinned its hopes on the BX as a middle ground between the small and large family car. The ZX represented a new approach from the French car maker and it offered a good spec, for a family car. Electric windows and sunroof, airbags and ABS were all fitted as standard or optional extras, providing excellent value for money when compared with the competition. However, the car was criticised for seeming cheap and plasticky and there were complaints concerning the quality of the interior trim and fittings. Despite this it sold well and the diesel-engined ZX was amongst the best in its class.

Another French manufacturer making waves during the 1990s was Peugeot. The **Peugeot 306**, which came to the market in 1993, shared the same floorplan as the Citroen ZX and was mechanically very similar, but proved to be a better seller. The 306 looked attractive, due to its Pininfarina-inspired design, came with a good variety of petrol engines and also an excellent diesel version was available. In 1997, the 306 was given an upgrade that offered new engine types, an improved dashboard and restyled bumpers. The 306 hatchback was discontinued in 2001, when it was replaced with the 307, but it had shown that Peugeot would be a force to be reckoned with in the years ahead.

By the end of the decade the small family car had become a major feature of most manufacturers' product ranges. Smaller cars were now able to offer all the advantages of

The Peugeot 306 was one of the best-looking cars in its class, and was great to drive as well.

their bigger rivals, with the added incentives of economy and value for money. By the end of the following decade, smaller cars had started to dominate the top ten bestseller list, proving that they were now the future of the traditional family car market.

Even now the Peugeot 306 doesn't look dated, thanks to its brilliant Pininfarina-inspired design.

SMALL FAMILY CARS OF THE 90S

1. Ford Escort MkV
2. Ford Escort RS Cosworth
3. Ford Focus
4. Vauxhall Astra MkIII and IV
5. Citroen ZX
6. Peugeot 306

Large Family Cars

The runaway success of the Escort and Astra meant that the larger section of the family car market suffered during the 1990s. The decade also saw the emergence of the MPV, which further diluted the desire for bigger cars. Nevertheless, the major manufacturers produced some good cars, but Rover was still making the same old mistakes.

The 400 was yet another unexceptional car from the Rover stable.

In Tourer (estate) form the Rover 400 was quite handsome, but wasn't innovative.

By the start of the 1990s the writing was definitely on the wall for the larger family car. But there was still room for these larger vehicles in the marketplace and Vauxhall's Cavalier and Ford's Mondeo sold well. Rover had experienced limited success with its 200 range and it had high hopes that the new 400 range would be able to compete with Vauxhall and Ford.

Released in 1990, the **Rover 400** was essentially just a saloon version of the 200 range. The car was designed in collaboration with Honda and it was derived from the popular Honda Civic. The 400 range was further updated in 1995 with a new design being based on the Honda Domani, which had been released in Japan three years earlier. Rover already marketed the Montego in the large family car sector and it placed the 400 in the same bracket. This was an error as the 400 wasn't really a big car. It was far more akin to the Astra and Escort in size and performance, but Rover hadn't

Rover had already marketed the Montego in the large family car sector

learned from the mistakes it had made with the 200. Despite this, the 400 initially had fairly good sales figures but, during the mid-90s, it soon fell out of favour and by the end of the decade it was not selling in any great quantities. Rover tried to arrest the decline by rebadging the 400 as the 45, in 1999. This time it aimed the car at the smaller sector by reducing the price and upping the basic specification, which saw a rise in its popularity, but it was too little too late and, once again, Rover had missed an opportunity.

The most popular large family car during the early 1990s was the **Vauxhall Cavalier**. The MkIII version of the long running Cavalier

The MkIII Vauxhall Cavalier was far more modern than the Ford Sierra, which is why it was a strong seller.

had been brought to market in 1988 and it sported a new, more modern and curvier style than its predecessor. From 1990 until 1994 it was the bestselling large family car in Britain and it was only ousted from its top spot with the release of Ford's Mondeo. The big advantage that the Cavalier had was that it was far newer than the Sierra, the other big name in the market, and while Ford developed the Mondeo it was the number one choice in the sector. To support the standard models Vauxhall released two powerful variants, starting with a new SRi version that was fitted with the same excellent 2-litre 8-valve engine from the previous generation's similar model. There was also a four-wheel drive GSi 2000 edition released, which helped to boost sales of the more staid family version. 1992 saw the high-end Cavalier further improved with the introduction of the Cavalier Turbo, which replaced the GSi2000 and could produce over 200bhp, but it was to be short-lived and it was cancelled with the introduction of the new Vectra, in 1995.

Even in the final year of the Cavalier's life it sold well in the UK, achieving almost 74,000 sales, but the time had come for a change and Vauxhall's new car would carry the Vectra badge, which the European versions of the Cavalier had held for several years. The **Vectra** built on the legacy of the Cavalier and brought an estate version to the UK market, something

The Vauxhall Vectra was always going to struggle to compete with the Mondeo.

The big advantage of the Cavalier was that it was far newer than the Sierra

that had been sorely lacking with the Cavalier range. It would prove to be a good seller for Vauxhall and countered the rise of the Sierra's replacement – the mighty Mondeo.

Ford had known that the Sierra would need replacing for quite some time. The foresight it had shown, in terms of the Sierra's curvy and futuristic design, had served it well and even though the car's sales figures had begun to decline, it kept Ford in the large family car market while the **Mondeo** was being developed. This was just as well, as the Mondeo was a major undertaking for Ford.

The Ford Mondeo was one of the most capacious estates around when it went on sale in 1993.

The American company had invested between five and a half and six billion dollars on the car's design, something that was necessary if Ford was to impose its dominance on the world stage. The car was designed for the world market and was new from the bottom up, sharing very little, if anything significant, with the anachronistic Sierra.

Priority was given to safety and interior specification in equal measures. Ford wanted a car that was reliable and safe enough to compete with the European giants, but also one that was pleasurable to travel in.

For an affordable front-wheel drive family car, the Ford Mondeo was amazingly good to drive.

The 405 was another great-looking car from Peugeot.

LARGE FAMILY CARS OF THE 90S

1. Rover 400
2. Vauxhall Cavalier
3. Vauxhall Vectra
4. Ford Mondeo
5. Volvo S80
6. Peugeot 405
7. Volkswagen Passat

Armrests, electric windows and central locking were just some of the refinements to be included and Ford ensured that a Ghia version was included in the range. Despite these touches the Mondeo was still seen as a bit bland, a criticism that had been levelled at the new Escort upon its release, too.

The Volvo S80 was a departure from the traditional, rather boxy, Volvo style.

The reality was that the larger car was a dying breed. Smaller cars were now more popular

To combat this a facelift was applied, in 1996, which improved on the Mondeo's looks and also addressed other problems with the MkI, such as lack of room in the back and poorly performing headlights. The Mondeo gradually gathered fans and sold well in the UK. The MkII further improved sales and even the then British Prime Minister, Tony Blair, bought a Mondeo, in 1997.

With Ford and Vauxhall slugging it out it was hard for other manufacturers to compete. The Swedish manufacturer, Volvo, released several models during the 1990s, including the **S80**, in 1998, which was declared 'the most beautiful car in the world' by the Italian car magazine, *Automobilia*. The **Peugeot 405** arrived at the end of the 1980s and continued to be refined through the 1990s. Volkswagen also tried to compete with its revised **Passat** but, despite regular updates, the car remained relatively expensive and it, too, couldn't really compete – although later on it would do so.

The reality was that the larger car was a dying breed. Smaller cars were now more popular and the larger size vehicles were having to compete with modern SUVs and the emergence of the MPV, both of which provided better value for money, or more of a status symbol, something that traditionally the larger car had always embodied. It was a sign of the times and at the end of the 1990s it was debatable as to whether or not the large family car had a future at all.

The Passat didn't sell well for Volkswagen in the 1990s, but a decade later it would prove incredibly popular.

For the first time in decades, there was a Bentley available that wasn't just a rebadged Rolls-Royce; the Continental R.

Luxury Cars

When it came to the ultimate in luxury the British still reigned supreme, but the Germans released some special cars during the 1990s and the Japanese also entered the market, bringing a new approach to the highest echelon of car design.

Having a luxury version of a mass-produced car was nothing new and by the 1990s the 'luxury' tag was fairly ubiquitous in the literature of manufacturers from Ford to Vauxhall. By now BMW and Mercedes had become seen as premium marques and even their basic models could be considered luxurious. But a true luxury car has no mass-produced version. These vehicles are deliberately a cut above the rest, bringing refinement and opulence to a select few.

The Continental R was perhaps the greatest grand tourer of its time.

The decade would produce some wonderful examples of the luxury car and at the forefront of the sector was the mighty Bentley.

Traditionally, Bentley had shared the body-shells of its cars with Rolls-Royce, but all that changed in 1992 with the innovative **Continental R**. In 1984, at the Geneva Motor Show, Bentley had shown off a concept car entitled Project 90. The prototype was for a new coupé Bentley and the concept model was received so well that Bentley set the wheels rolling on production – and eight years later the Continental R was the result. Bentley knew it was on to a winner when, at the Geneva Motor Show of 1991, the Sultan of Brunei purchased the bright red display model on the spot.

'To build a good car, a fast car, the best in its class'

W. O. Bentley

The Continental R was far more rounded in style than the previous generations of Bentleys and it featured seamless, roof-cut doors and an almost imperceptible rear spoiler. The dream-machine was powered by a 6.75-litre Garrett-turbocharged engine capable of supplying over 320bhp to the driver's right foot, which slammed the giant machine to 60mph in just 6.5 seconds and was capable of

Those wanting the wind in their hair could buy an open Continental R, in the form of the Azure.

a top speed of 145mph. The limited edition version, produced in 1994 and 1995, was even quicker. The Continental S, as it was termed, shaved half a second off the 0–60 time, but only 37 of these attractive monsters were ever produced.

Inside, the Continental R was the height of finery and sophistication. Deep carpets, soft-hide leather seats, a bar, a television, sound-proofing and wood finishes made the interior of the car more like a penthouse apartment than a vehicle. All this luxury came at a price though, and a new Continental R cost £200,000 in 1995, which was an awful lot of money. It was difficult to see how Bentley could have improved on the Continental R, but for those who wanted more speed there was the Continental T, which sacrificed some of the refinement for more pace, although not much, and there was also the breathtaking **Bentley Azure**.

The Azure was the title given to the convertible version of the Continental R. It took over two years to refine the prototype and Bentley sought the assistance of Pininfarina in the design process. By the time production began the Azure's intercooled Garrett-turbocharged engine was capable of outputting 385bhp, giving the car a 0–60 time of 6.3 seconds and a top speed of 150mph. The Azure and the Continental R were the absolute pinnacle of automotive luxury, but if the price tag was a bit steep there were plenty of other options.

The BMW 8-Series was very advanced but costly, and many didn't warm to its looks.

BMW's 850CSi represented the very zenith of sports-touring luxury. The CSi was the top line version of the 8 Series, which represented the German manufacturer's flagship range. The 850CSi's engine modified the standard 850's 5.6-litre powerplant to produce a whopping 375bhp that was ably tamed by the

The 8-Series offered room for four, making it a superb long-distance tourer.

The W140 series S-Class was perhaps the most refined saloon available when it was launched.

six-speed gearbox. The European versions of the CSi featured an innovative four-wheel steering system, which massively improved the car's handling and performance. In the end, European emissions laws dulled the car's potential and, in 1999, BMW dropped it from the range.

It was boxy and ugly, but the W140 S-Class was a technological marvel, packing some amazing engineering.

BMW's 850CSi represented the zenith of sports-touring luxury

Not to be outdone, Mercedes had its own luxury powerhouse during the 1990s in the form of the **W140 S-Class**. The W140 was larger than its predecessor and further refined the S-Class, but this came at a price with the W140 costing an average of 25 per cent more than the W126. Even so, the owner of a W140 S-Class got a lot for their money. The new car came with a self-closing boot, double-glazed

The W220 S-Class was far more attractive than its W140 predecessor – and even more advanced.

windows and parking sensors, on top of the usual, opulent fare. In 1999, the S-Class was further redefined by the **W220**, which featured such luxuries as seats that contained small fans for ventilation when things got hot, keyless entry and a voice-activated navigation system. Despite these touches the car wasn't well received and some critics referred to the W220 as the least reliable luxury car ever made.

The Germans needed to be good as during the decade a new challenger appeared in the form of the Japanese manufacturer, Lexus. Lexus is the luxury car division of Toyota

The LS400 could reach 60mph in 8 seconds, thanks to a powerful 4-litre engine

and in 1989 it proved it was serious with the release of the outstanding **LS400**. Costing more than $1bn to develop, the LS400 offered a new approach to the luxury car. The Japanese manufacturer wanted to surpass the standards of the European luxury car makers on every level. The LS400 was only available on limited release in the UK, as Lexus was still finding its feet, but the car was such a success that future models would be released worldwide. The LS400 could reach 60mph in 8 seconds, thanks to a powerful 4-litre engine and had a top speed of 160mph. In terms of luxury fittings, the car boasted airbags, walnut trim and leather upholstery, electronic memory systems for seat positions and a host of other refinements. The car was aimed at

The W220 S-Class packed in the technology, but it wasn't always reliable.

Lexus put the cat among the pigeons when it launched the LS400. It offered unsurpassed refinement, technology and reliability in the luxury sector.

LUXURY CARS OF THE 90S

1. Bentley Continental R
2. Bentley Azure
3. BMW 850CSi
4. Mercedes W140 S-Class
5. Mercedes W220 S-Class
6. Lexus LS400

beating the BMW 735i and the Mercedes 420SE and it did so, with ease. It was faster, quieter and avoided the heavy tax imposed in the United States on powerful cars. During the 1990s the LS400 was further refined and by the end of the decade Lexus was firmly a part of the luxury car set.

The British had proved that they were still the best at making the top-line in luxury, but these cars were never going to sell in bulk. But that didn't matter. They were meant to be exclusive. BMW and Mercedes had the next level down sewn up but, by the end of the 1990s, they were playing catch up to the Japanese. Lexus had shown there was another way of building luxury cars. Over the coming years, East and West were to go head-to-head, and the next generation of luxury, and just about affordable, cars would prove to be beyond the wildest dreams of mortal men.

Cameras and culture: life and death

Between 1966 and 1994 the number of cars on British roads had doubled to 25 million. There was also a rise in safety standards. Anti-lock disc brakes, airbags and structural systems all enabled people to drive faster, and with more confidence. In 1966 the number of fatal accidents on Britain's roads was almost 8,000 a year and although by 1993 the number had halved, it was still a major problem. The most alarming thing was that despite the advances in road and car safety the fall in the number of fatal crashes had slowed.

Speed cameras

What caused this decline? To many, it was the introduction of the very thing that was meant to make the roads safer; the speed camera. In 1992, the first 'safety' or 'speed' cameras were installed in West London, triggering a shift in policing policy. No longer would the police patrol the roads of Britain in such numbers. Now it was machinery that would keep Britain's drivers in check, but these autonomous machines, and their mass implementation, had a major flaw. They were only capable of registering a car's speed; they couldn't observe drink driving, lane indiscipline or driver fatigue. As the majority of the cameras were in fixed positions, it didn't take long for people to know where they were. Drivers would simply slow down when they approached a camera, speeding up once they had passed, safe in the

Top: Speed cameras sprung up everywhere in the 1990s.
Centre: These yellow 'Gatsos' were hated by most drivers.
Bottom: Drivers were lucky to find an open stretch of road.

knowledge that there was unlikely to be a policeman around the corner, waiting to pounce.

Excessive speed, driven by 80s car culture, was certainly an issue. During trials on the M40, in the early 90s, cameras were using up their entire film of 400 photos in under 40 minutes; it was clear that speeding was a problem. By 1997, the government was spending almost £4 million a year on anti-speeding advertising, and cameras across the country were accounting for almost £100 million in fines; but people weren't slowing down.

Culture suceeds where technology failed

Ultimately, what slowed down traffic on British roads were changes in society and car culture. The British penchant for speed was being replaced by a shift back to traditional values, called for by the new government, and reflected by the car manufacturers. Perhaps the best example of this can be seen in the rise of the MPV, or as it is better known, the people carrier. Released in 1996, the Renault Scenic was voted European Car of the Year in 1997 and it was to be the first of many of this new type of vehicle. The MPV stood for family values; it was economical, seated seven people and stressed comfort and safety over speed. After all, what was the point of a family crammed into a fast car, on congested roads full of speed cameras?

The MPV signalled a shift in car design that continues to be seen today. Not so much in terms of the MPV itself, but in manufacturers highlighting comfort, economy and practicality above all else. This enabled the further development of hybrid and electric cars, where speed and power were not the defining attributes. By the end of the decade, the MPV ethos had slowed down speeds on the country's highways, making roads safer and managing what the 'safety camera' could not.

Top: The Renault Scenic was the first compact MPV.
Centre: The Scenic focused on practicality, not speed.
Bottom: The Scenic would lead to a large glut of rivals.

It's unlikely that there will ever again be a supercar as pure as the McLaren F1.

Sports Cars

At the beginning of the 1990s motor manufacturers were worried that there could be another oil crisis on the horizon. Iraq had invaded Kuwait and the Middle East was looking as volatile as it had been for the last 20 years. After the resurgence of the 1980s this did not bode well. As it happened, the world united and Kuwait was liberated in a matter of days. By the middle of the decade prosperity had returned, the sports car was alive and well and the 1990s was to bring some truly awesome machines. The decade was to give the world the Dodge Viper, Jaguar XJ220, Ferrari F50 and the earth shattering McLaren F1.

After what seemed like an eternity in the wilderness, a British car manufacturer was about to take the world by storm. McLaren

During the 1990s, in the world of the supercar, Britain would reign supreme as McLaren taught the European giants how to hit 240mph. But, in terms of the road-going sports car, Audi would unveil a car that quite literally reshaped ideas of design and style. Sports cars were now cooler than ever before.

was already a well respected and well developed Formula 1 team, but it was about to release a road car that would, some would say, never be bettered. Designed by Gordon Murray, who already created Formula 1 cars for Brabham and McLaren, the F1 would utilise Formula 1 technology to propel the car into automotive legend.

The **McLaren F1** was unveiled in Monaco in 1993, the night before the jewel in the crown of the racing calendar. Powered by a

The McLaren F1 was completely uncompromised, but it was hugely expensive as a result.

McLaren was first and foremost a motorsport company, so it knew all about building seriously fast cars.

'The F1 will be remembered as one of the great events in the history of the car' *Autocar*

V12 6-litre engine, the F1 could attain a top speed of 240mph! Considering that the F1 was released just seven years after the F40, it's remarkable that the Ferrari's top speed of 201mph was so utterly trumped. McLaren declared that 300 F1s would be produced costing a cool £540,000 apiece, but by the time the car went out of production, in 1997, only 100 had been built, including racers – the price tag doubtless having something to do with the shortfall in demand.

The F1 was unique in so many ways and this contributed to its status. The car featured a central driver's seat with two passengers sat behind. It sported the same scissor doors that had been so unique on Lamborghini's Countach; it even had giant sucking devices mounted under the car to increase down-force. The F1 had real racing pedigree, too. In 1994, a GTR version was built which won the 1995 and 1996 World Championships and dominated the 1995 Le Mans race, taking 1st, 3rd, 4th and 13th places in the gruelling 24-hour endurance challenge.

The McLaren F1 may well have been the definitive supercar of the 1990s, but it was by no means the only super-fast sports car. After the success of the F40, Ferrari was quick to build on the impressive foundations, with

The F50 was the successor to the F40; it was created to celebrate 50 years of Ferrari building cars.

The Dodge Viper was a completely mad brute of a machine, with an 8-litre V10 engine.

the F50. The **F50**, like the F40, was built to commemorate the company's anniversary; like McLaren's wonder car, the F50 was based on Formula 1 technology. The F50 was the most powerful Ferrari ever produced but its top speed of 202mph left it trailing in McLaren's wake. The F50 was powered by a 4.7-litre V12 capable of producing 513bhp and propelling the car to 60mph in just 3.7 seconds. Like the F40, the F50 was sparse inside with the dashboard consisting of just a speedometer and rev counter mounted in an LCD box. The F50 went into production in 1995 and by the 50th anniversary 349 units had been produced, ensuring that Ferrari kept its head above water in the age of the McLaren F1.

Along with Ferrari and McLaren's super-cars there were two other notable models that emerged in the 1990s; the Jaguar XJ220 and the Dodge Viper. The **Jaguar XJ220** was released just before the McLaren F1 and for a while, at least, it held the mantle of the world's fastest production car. With a top speed of 213mph it showed that Jaguar's racing pedigree was still alive and well and that the manufacturer could still compete on the world supercar stage. The car featured with some success at Le Mans, but at a cost of £361,000 each (twice the price of Ferrari's F40) it was too expensive and too niche to really be a huge success.

Dodge also entered the fray with its second generation **Viper**. The car had begun life as a concept car, but was received with such acclaim at its unveiling that it went into full production, in 1992. Further improved upon a year later with the release of the GTS version, the Viper, thanks to its new 450bhp engine, was capable of reaching speeds of 170mph.

The Jaguar XJ220 was a fabulous machine, but it was far too costly to be truly competitive.

Despite its speed the Viper suffered from steering and handling issues that American supercar manufacturers have never really been able to overcome. However, it did show that the Europeans were not the only people capable of creating very fast and highly desirable cars. It also showed that the roadster was capable of much more than it had been in the past.

The Toyota Supra showed you could have massive performance with superb reliability.

Away from the world of supercars the 1990s also saw the inception of some classic mainstream sports cars. **Toyota's Supra** started life as a version of the already successful Celica coupé and through the years consistently developed until the final version of the car was released, in 1993. Powered by a twin-turbocharged six-cylinder engine the car's speed was limited to 155mph and it was capable of 0–60 in around 5 seconds. It looked like a road car, but had racing lines and kept the Japanese in the fast car market.

Subaru's **Impreza WRX STi** improved on the existing Impreza, but upped the power considerably to a whopping 240bhp. In 1995, the car, driven by Colin McRae, gave Subaru its first World Rally Championship. It was to win the title for the next two years as it dominated the world rally scene. These titles and the 2,500 road car versions built for homologation purposes, ensured that the Impreza proved popular both on and off the track.

In 1995, the car, driven by Colin McRae, gave Subaru its first World Rally Championship

The final sports car of the 1990s that merits a mention in our list is the iconic **Audi TT**. On its unveiling as a concept car at the 1995 Frankfurt Motor Show it was clear that Audi had built a generation-defining machine. The TT's lines were distinctive, as it looked quite unlike any other sports car currently on the road. The reception was so positive that Audi went into production and the road version of the TT coupé was released at the 1998 Paris Motor Show. The basic model TT produced an impressive 180bhp, rocketing the little car to a top speed of 140mph along with equally notable acceleration statistics of 0–60 in a shade over 7 seconds. The roadster version of the coupé soon followed and by the turn of the decade over 100,000 units had been produced. The TT combined class with style, old with new and it set the scene for the future of the modern sports car.

The 1990s was a notable decade in the development of the sports car. The McLaren F1, Jaguar XJ220 and Ferrari F50 pushed the abilities of the supercar to the limits of technology. But in the world of more popular cars, the Audi TT, BMW 5-Series and Renault Clio Sport V6 pushed the boundaries of what it was possible to achieve on a budget. As the turn of the century approached, the future of the sports car had never looked brighter.

Audi unveiled the TT in concept form and decided to put it into production. The rest is history.

SPORTS CARS OF THE 90S

1. McLaren F1
2. Dodge Viper
3. Jaguar XJ220
4. Ferrari F50
5. Toyota Supra
6. Subaru Impreza WRX STi
7. Audi TT

The second-generation Range Rover was even more luxurious than the first, but horrifically unreliable.

SUVs

Land Rover had given birth to the modern SUV during the 1970s and over the course of the 1990s it would experience a rapid transformation from 4x4 to status symbol. Many other companies could see the potential of the SUV and, love them or hate them, the SUVs were here to stay.

The SUV was always going to be a controversial vehicle. Its heritage dictated that things such as fuel consumption and engine emissions were not going to be priorities when it came to design. These modern vehicles were born from the wild where power and size were essential factors in their survival. But how important were these assets on the road and around the congested streets of the country's cities and towns? Surely modern, urban driving demanded the opposite skill-set to that of the SUV; cars should be nippy, efficient, clean and small. But, at the start of the 1990s, there was one company that was determined to prove this hypothesis wrong, and that was Land Rover.

These modern vehicles were born from the wild where their power and size were essential

The British 4x4 maker had been the benchmark for 4x4s for decades and when it introduced the Range Rover, in 1970, it had stumbled onto a new breed of car. The Range Rover had proved that there was a place for the 4x4 in the British, urban environment and, in 1989, Land Rover decided to see just how popular the SUV could become when it released the **Land Rover Discovery**.

The Discovery was based on the Range Rover's chassis and drivetrain, but Land Rover wanted to aim it at the mass-market, so the price was lowered and the spec was toned down. Land Rover knew that in order for

The Discovery was just as well-loved as the Range Rover – but it was every bit as unreliable too.

Anyone buying a second-generation Range Rover had to settle for a five-door bodyshell as there was no three-door.

the Discovery to work it would have to be marketed very carefully and, accordingly, they employed the Conran Design Group to model the interior of the car. The instruction to the designers was to create not just a car, but a lifestyle accessory – something that people would need, not just want. The result was a success and the car was critically acclaimed. The new style interior was only available in light blue and featured such additions as removable sunroof panels, map holding slots above the windscreen, remote radio controls and very 4x4 looking handrails, for when the

The last-of-the-line second-generation Range Rover looked very slick, but the third-generation car was much better.

BMW proved with its X5 that a large SUV can be fun to drive.

asphalt got a bit bumpy. Despite the acclaim that the Discovery received, most of the interior fittings were standard fare and could be found on the Range Rover and even on the Montego and Maestro.

In 1992, improvements were made to the range and beige was now added as a choice of interior colour. Further improvements were made in 1994; new engines were installed and the new 2.5-litre TDI 5-cylinder and 3.9-litre V8s were a big improvement on the original powerhouses. The Series II Discovery was unveiled at the end of 1988 and the new generation further softened the traditional ideas of a 4x4. It was less workmanlike in appearance and by the end of the decade it had forced its way into the family car market, in true bullish 4x4 style.

The granddaddy of the 4x4 was, by the mid-1990s, beginning to show its age

Land Rover's Range Rover, the granddaddy of the 4x4, was by the mid-nineties beginning to show its age and the success of the Discovery meant that a newer version was required. This came in 1994 with the arrival of the **Range Rover MkII**. The looks had been refined and a new engine option – a BMW 2.5-litre, six-cylinder turbodiesel – was

BMW didn't hold back when it was engineering the X5, which is why this large SUV was so good to drive.

In 1995, BMW launched the X5, a crossover vehicle designed to compete with the Range Rover

added to the range. The new Rover had some groundbreaking technology, such as automatic height adjustment, to ensure adequate ground clearance (which in the end proved expensive to maintain) and there was also the release of a luxury model, the HSE. The **Range Rover HSE** elevated the SUV to the kind of luxury status it enjoys today. An excellent Harmon Kardon sound system, headrest DVD players, satellite navigation and large alloy wheels all made the Range Rover truly luxurious, and the HSE paved the way for the upmarket Vogue, which was released at the turn of the century. Land Rover had succeeded in getting two vehicles into the SUV market, with great success, but other manufacturers had been watching with interest, and they soon joined the fray.

In 1999, BMW launched the **X5**, a crossover that was designed to compete with the Range Rover and Discovery, but was always more a car than a traditional SUV. If the desert was your destination then a Range Rover or Land Rover was still the prime choice. But, if your port of call was Harrods or Harvey Nichols, then BMW wanted you to take the X5. It was an SUV that was designed for urban driving and this could be seen in the X5's design. Most of the power was engineered to go through the rear wheels, giving the feel of a 5 or 7-Series as opposed to a rugged 4x4. But it was still capable of four-wheel drive performance and by 1999 BMW owned Land Rover, so it was able to take advantage of the existing technology. The interior of the X5 came straight from the 5-Series of the day and premium quality was essential for the X5 to succeed. From the off, BMW wanted the car to be known as an SAV or Sports Activity Vehicle, to distinguish it from the Range Rover and also account for the lack of real 4x4 capabilities.

SUVS OF THE 90S

1. Land Rover Discovery
2. Range Rover MkII
3. Range Rover HSE
4. BMW X5
5. Mercedes ML-Class

Mercedes entered the large SUV market with its ML-Class, but it missed the mark thanks to poor build quality.

Unlike many full-size SUVs the Mercedes ML was designed to be taken off road.

Mercedes, too, was quick to follow suit and release its own SUV and, in 1997, it launched the **ML-Class**. Like the X5, the ML was a crossover SUV and was designed more for the road than the wilds. It featured all of Mercedes' usual safety devices and was equipped with an electronic stability system, to bring the huge car back under control if things got tricky. A 2.7-litre turbodiesel powered the standard ML 270CDI model and in 1999 a 4.3-litre version was released. The ML sold well and Mercedes was smart with its marketing, ensuring that the vehicles appeared in the blockbuster movie, *Jurassic Park: The Lost World*, further increasing awareness. Initially there were concerns over the quality of the ML and it received less than favourable reviews, particularly from *Top Gear*, but things would improve with later generations.

By the end of the 1990s the future of the SUV was assured and it had carved itself out a niche that lay somewhere between the large family and luxury car sectors. In effect, the SUV was becoming the new large family car and as the new century beckoned more and more manufacturers would release their own versions of the sports utility vehicle.

Renault was the first European car maker to offer an MPV, but it was the Chrysler Voyager that started it all.

MPVs

The 1990s witnessed the meteoric rise of the MPV, or Multi Purpose Vehicle. The MPV was becoming the modern version of the large family car, offering space and comfort for the larger family in a way that traditional cars could not, and by the end of the decade most of the major manufacturers had their own versions on the market.

It was during the 1950s that the humble van first showed potential for the passenger market. Volkswagen's classic Type 2, soon to be loved by surfers all over the world, took the first steps into the realm of the car not long after the end of World War II and as over the proceeding decades the car market fractured into multiple sectors, the MPV began to take on the mantle of the large family car.

The third-generation Espace was a far sleeker MPV than the first-generation edition.

After the full-size Espace MPV came the Megane Scenic; the first compact MPV.

The first European MPV was the **Renault Espace**, which made its debut in the mid-1980s. The Espace had a fairly inauspicious start and only sold a reported nine units in the first month of production, but soon things changed and the Espace was to set the tone for the modern MPV. By the early 1990s Renault had produced the Espace II, which debuted in 1991. Although the chassis was unchanged from the original model, it was refined internally, which made it more appealing to the mass market. The Espace III, which followed in 1997, made further improvements and added touches such as a digital speedometer and a central dashboard. Up to this point the Espace had been built by the French company, Matra, but marketed as a Renault product, and the third generation of the Espace would be Matra's last model before Renault took over Espace production in its entirety. The Espace drove like a car, but could accommodate multiple occupants. It also benefitted from the usual high standard of safety features expected of Renault and proved that there was a future for these larger vehicles.

'This is the Renault Espace, the best of the people carriers'
Jeremy Clarkson

In 1996, Renault took the concept of the MPV even further when it announced the **Scenic**, a compact version of the Espace. The chassis was based on the Mégane and just one year after its release it was voted European Car of the Year, in 1997.

The success of the Scenic took Renault by surprise. The company envisaged that it would be popular, but before long the factory was producing some 2,500 Scenics a day – five times the predicted number. For the first two years of the Scenic's life it was the only real compact MPV on the market, but within five years Vauxhall and Citroen had released their own versions.

One of the most popular competitors to the Scenic was Citroen's **Xsara Picasso**. Unveiled in 1999, it soon became the bestselling MPV in France and the UK and would continue to develop during the following decade. The Picasso was based on the existing Xsara, a small family car, and part of the Picasso's attraction was that it drove just like its smaller sibling, attracting customers who had been put off by the size of the early MPVs.

The Xsara Picasso proved to be a smash hit for Citroen.

Around the same time, Vauxhall showed off its own compact MPV, in the shape of the **Zafira**. It was based on the same platform as the 1988 Astra and again embodied the characteristics of a small car. Vauxhall incorporated what it termed as Flex 7 into the Zafira's design. This clever technology

While some compact MPVs were available with up to seven seats, the Xsara Picasso came with only five.

The Zafira was based on the Astra, but could seat seven. It was the first MPV to feature fold-flat seats.

Over the years, Ford had experienced a great deal of success with its large cars

and use of space enabled the Zafira to seat seven, two of whom would have to be children due to the lack of legroom. This use of space put it ahead of the competition and showed that a relatively small vehicle could be almost Tardis-like, melding space and practicality like never before. The first iteration of the Zafira suffered from ride problems and tended to roll on corners, but this was improved upon in later models. Like the Citroen and Renault models, the Zafira was safe, comfortable and frugal, but its size meant it could be rather noisy on motorways; perhaps a small price to pay for the overall package, and certainly it didn't seem to bother the public, who queued up to buy it.

Over the years, Ford had experienced a great deal of success with its large cars. The Cortina had been untouchable in the large car sector and the Sierra and Mondeo had also been good sellers. But the large family car market had stagnated somewhat and the American giant was keen to ensure that it didn't miss the MPV boat. In 1995, Ford announced the **Galaxy**, a large MPV, which was developed in co-operation with Volkswagen, which was also keen to enter the MPV market. Accordingly, the Galaxy was badge-engineered to create **Volkswagen's Sharan** and also the **SEAT Alhambra**.

The Volkswagen Sharan was built in conjunction with Ford, which sold it as the Galaxy.

MPVS OF THE 90S

1. Renault Espace
2. Renault Scenic
3. Citroen Xsara Picasso
4. Vauxhall Zafira
5. Ford Galaxy
6. Volkswagen Sharan
7. SEAT Alhambra

The petrol-engined Galaxy was powered by the same 2.8-litre engine that was found in Volkswagen's Golf VR6 and there was also a 1.9-litre turbodiesel option. Inside, the Galaxy was fairly sparse, especially when compared with the Zafira and Scenic, but the Galaxy was always intended to be more functional. It soon became a favourite with taxi firms and in 2000 a MkII version was released, although it was still available with Sharan or Alhambra badges. The Galaxy didn't receive great reviews though. A *Top Gear* survey of 1999 voted it the least satisfying car in the UK, but Ford pressed on with the Galaxy and resisted the urge to change the vehicle's size.

Since the 1960s car design had been moving towards smaller and leaner models, which were more economical to run and practical to use in ever denser traffic.

Predictably, of the three variants on offer, it was the Ford Galaxy which sold in the greatest numbers.

This had affected the large family car sector the most but the MPV somewhat bucked the trend. Renault had shown that the consumer still liked the idea of space and that for the larger family a car such as the Escort was not really big enough.

The MPV didn't really get going until the end of the 1990s but, within a very short space of time, it had managed to assert itself on the British public. By the end of the following decade the compact MPV was even making waves in the smaller family car sector and had become a very common sight on the roads of Britain.

'The car market, like the political landscape, is vastly changed'

Guardian review of the VW Sharan

As well as the Galaxy and Sharan, SEAT also offered this full-size MPV as the Alhambra.

2000s

10 Bestsellers

By the start of the 2000s the car had come a long way from its humble beginnings. There was now a multitude of car classes available, representing more choice than ever before for the consumer. The car was also much more affordable than it had ever been, which in turn enabled car manufacturers to offer a seemingly endless array of add-ons, from satellite navigation systems to prefabricated racing modifications.

During the decade, the gap between rich and poor grew ever more prominent and car makers were quick to capitalise. In the luxury sector Rolls-Royce would continue to produce some of the finest cars the world had ever seen and German manufacturers, such as BMW, Mercedes and Audi would continue to offer the car buyer that little something extra.

The biggest change would come courtesy of the SUV, or Sports Utility Vehicle. These cars would not only court controversy, with their polluting credentials, but would also spell disaster for the traditional large family car. The smaller family car would get steadily more efficient, culminating in the advent of the compact MPV that could offer the space of a larger car, in a smaller shell.

Sports cars would continue to excel and a new super-model, from Bugatti, would challenge Ferrari, Porsche and Lamborghini for the fastest road car. Superminis would also further develop and the 2000s would see the reincarnation of an old favourite; the Mini would return, better than ever and ready to conquer the world again.

of the 2000s

1.

• STATS AND FACTS •

FOCUSED POWER
The fastest Focus ever made was the 2009 Focus RS MkII. Its engine produced 301bhp and catapulted the car to 164mph, with a 0–60 time of just 5.8 seconds.

A CLOSE CALL
In Germany, a magazine claimed the rights to the Focus name but, luckily for Ford, an agreement was reached and the car was released in Germany.

Focus buyers had a choice of three or five-door hatchbacks, a four-door saloon or a five-door estate.

Ford Focus

Since the 1970s, Ford's Escort had been a permanent fixture in the top ten sales charts in the UK. In the 1980s it was the bestselling car in the country, but by the 1990s it had started to lose ground on the Fiesta, and the competition. It was time for a change and Ford's answer was the Focus.

Released in 1998, Ford continued the styling trend of the Ka and Cougar models and applied smooth and sweeping lines to the new Focus. The car was fitted with the trusty Zetec engine range and it was built to meet the new European safety criteria; receiving four out of five stars for occupant safety in Euro NCAP crash tests. The Focus handled well and benefited from a sophisticated, fully independent, multi-link rear suspension system, which gave it an excellent ride.

The Focus was available in a three or five-door hatchback, four-door saloon and five-door estate versions and there were also performance models in the shape of the ST170 and RS models. The Focus was a good seller and Ford was quick to capitalise on its popularity. In 2004, the second-generation model was revealed at the Paris Motor Show. The new generation was very similar to the first with the major changes being to the bodyshell's weight and size. The new car was also larger than its predecessor, allowing for greater interior space.

A speedy, second-generation MkII was also released, in 2005. It was the new Focus ST and it was the XR of its day, producing 225bhp and a top speed of 152mph along with a 0–60 time of just 6.4 seconds. This boded well for the car's racing credentials and it was an immediate success on the world rally scene. The Focus' maiden victory was achieved at the hands of Colin McRae in the 1999 Safari Rally. This was just the start and McRae again drove the Focus to victory in the Portugal Rally later that year. It was to be a continuing trend.

The Focus had proved in a short space of time that it was a car for the long-term

The Focus had proved in a short space of time that it was a car for the long-term. With rally credentials as well as notable handling on the average road, it is no surprise that the Focus remains the class-leader to this day.

The Focus ST packed a turbocharged 2.5-litre five-cylinder engine.

2. Vauxhall Astra

Over the previous decade the Astra had shown how good it was and began to threaten the status of the venerable Escort. The creation of the Focus was, in large part, due to the emergence of the Astra and with Ford's new world-beater in place, the pressure was on Vauxhall to keep the Astra at the top of its game.

The MkIV Astra had sold well and taken the marque through to the new century, but it was time for a change – next to the new Focus the Astra was beginning to look dated. The MkV Astra was unveiled at the beginning of 2004 to great acclaim. It was heralded as the best Astra yet and along with the Insignia, Clio and the company's MPV range, Vauxhall could now offer highly regarded vehicles across the entire spectrum.

By the end of the decade over 2.5 million Astras had been sold since the car's inception.

• STATS AND FACTS •

RISING POPULARITY

By 2001, the MkIV Astra was the 26th most popular car in the world, with the combined sales figures of both the Vauxhall and Opel versions totalling 3.8 million units.

DRIVING RESULTS

The MkV Astra was Britain's bestselling car in 2005, 2006 and 2007, showing that Ford had some serious competition for its Focus.

This made it the fourth most popular car in British motoring history. By the end of 2010 the Astra was finally outselling the Ford Focus. It was an impressive achievement for Vauxhall and highlighted how far the company had come in its mission to challenge the once dominant Ford.

The Astra sold well; this is a MkIV edition. It came in saloon, hatchback or estate configurations, while there was a convertible too.

Vauxhall has always done well in the UK with its smaller models; the third-generation Corsa was its best yet.

3. Vauxhall Corsa

Throughout the 1990s the Corsa had built well on the Nova's foundations. It had showed that Vauxhall was a serious competitor to Ford and by the 1990s it was outselling the Fiesta. In 1999, the C version was released, seeing the little car through until 2006. The C version sold extremely well; between 2002 and 2004 it was the second bestselling car in the country and in 2005 it achieved the status of the best-selling supermini in Britain. But, by the end of 2006, the Fiesta had regained the edge and in response Vauxhall released the D variant. In 2007, *What Car?* awarded the Corsa D Car of the Year. It received a five-star rating in Euro NCAP safety tests and was available with a range of economical engines, providing a safe car that suited the small family, and one that could compete again with the Fiesta. From the first Corsa to the present day, sales have achieved more than 1.5 million units, and that shows no signs of stopping. In 2010 the Corsa D received a facelift and still features in Vauxhall's line-up today.

• STATS AND FACTS •

CUDDLY CAR

In 2006, Vauxhall began using stuffed toys to advertise its new Corsa, but the muppets were not as popular in the UK as they were in Europe.

HIDDEN TALENTS

In Brazil, a pick-up truck version of the Corsa is available, named the Chevrolet Montana, proving the little car has plenty of hidden strength.

4. Ford Fiesta

In 2002 the all-new MkV hit the streets and it was to become the bestselling Fiesta so far. Improved dashboard design and high quality fitments on the inside matched new light designs, mouldings and bumpers on the outside. The MkV was also given some snazzy new technology such as a Bluetooth kit, automatic wipers and a trip computer. The new tricks worked and by 2006 the Fiesta had begun to outsell the Corsa again. The Fiesta just refused to be beaten.

• STATS AND FACTS •

SAMBA OLD STORY
Between the end of 2002 and the middle of 2007 some 336,000 Fiestas were sold in Brazil and the car continues to sell about 5,000 units a month.

VANTASTIC
All six generations of the Fiesta have been available in a panel van format. These provide an excellent mini-alternative to the larger Ford Transit vans.

5. VW Golf

The Golf was born in 1974 and by the year 2000 the car was on its fourth generation. The Golf has always been popular, but the price tag meant it was never going to outsell its rivals. In 2004 Volkswagen introduced an R32 version, fitted with a 3.2-litre VR6 engine delivering 0–60 in less than 6 seconds. The MkV Golf was available from 2004 and a MkVI arrived before the end of the decade. The Golf was now cheaper and better able to compete with the Focus and Astra.

• STATS AND FACTS •

HEIR TO THE THRONE
Volkswagen's Golf has had some famous owners, but perhaps none so famous as Kate Middleton – Duchess of Cambridge and the future Queen of England.

RUN RABBIT RUN
In the United States and Canada the Golf is known as the Volkswagen Rabbit. Naming models after animals is common paractice in the America market.

6. Peugeot 206

Peugeot backed away from the supermini market in the 1990s, but the success of the Fiesta and Corsa made it obvious they were missing out. The 206 was released in 1998 and replaced in 2006 by the 207. The 206 sold remarkably well and even though it was only available for half the decade it still fared well against the competition. It was available in many varieties, catering for a wide range of buyers. With the 206 Peugeot showed that they were now serious about the small car.

• STATS AND FACTS •

SLOW STARTER
By 2010, the 206 was Peugeot's bestselling car of all time, proving that although it took a while to catch up, Peugeot's forte is the small car.

BONJOUR
The Peugeot 206 was the best selling car in the whole of Europe, from 2001 to 2003. The 206 was as common on the streets of London as on the boulevards of France.

The Fiesta brand was familiar, but Ford kept it at the top of the supermini class.

Despite its relatively high price, buyers queued up for a VW Golf.

The 206 was popular because it was cheap, practical and well equipped.

The Mégane's rear-end styling was an acquired taste.

The third edition of the Clio looked more grown up than ever.

7. Renault Mégane

Introduced in 1995, the Mégane sold steadily and by the 2000s it had become a popular sight in the UK. The Mégane stood for safety and when, in 2002, the Mégane II was launched, it continued in the same vein. The new version received a five-star award from Euro NCAP and was voted European Car of the Year in 2003. However, the new Mégane was a completely different car from the first. The Mégane II had the famous protruding rear end, which was highlighted in Renault's advertising campaign, although the third generation, released in 2008, restyled the back of the car to make it more conventional.

• STATS AND FACTS •

HIGH FLYER
The Mégane's distinctive nose was borrowed from the famous 'bird-beak' design of the 1960s Renault 16. It is not known what the famous rear end was modelled on.

MOT PROUD
In 2007, the Mégane had the highest first MOT failure rate of any car in the UK, something which Renault was not very proud of.

8. Renault Clio

By the year 2000, the Clio had been in production for ten years. Since launch the car had sold very well across Europe and, to date, it is the only car to have been voted European Car of the Year twice; in 1991 and 2006. The Clio MkII was released in 1998 and brought a new, European style to the little city car. In 2006 the MkIII was launched to great acclaim. The Clio was able to compete with the Fiesta and Corsa on cost, performance and style and the Sports version was a serious speedster, producing 197bhp and a top speed of 141mph. The battle of the superminis was raging and the Clio was a serious contender.

• STATS AND FACTS •

AN UNWELCOME SURPRISE
In 2006 it was noted that a number of Clio MkIIs suffered from their bonnets flying open while the car was in motion.

VA VA VOOM
The advertising campaign for the Clio II featured the Arsenal and France footballer, Thierry Henry and coined the phrase 'Va va voom!'

The MkIII Mondeo was the biggest yet, and still great to drive.

9. Ford Mondeo

Despite the fact that the Mondeo is a very well built car, in the 2000s the era of the large family car was coming to an end. The Focus and Astra represented better value for money in a smaller car that was still adequate for the family. The MkIII Mondeo came to the market in 2000 and was well received. Some criticised its rather plain nature, but in terms of drive and build quality there were no complaints. New Duratec engines were installed and the MkIV, released in 2007, continued the successful formula. The Mondeo is still a top seller and part of Ford's present line-up; it shows no signs of stopping soon.

• STATS AND FACTS •

CLEVER CARS
The latest Mondeos feature clever technology such as headlights that automatically dip for oncoming traffic.

A DYING BREED
Between 2000 and 2007 the Mondeo was the bestselling family car in Britain. The big car may not be as popular as it once was, but the Mondeo does the job well.

The 3-Series has long set the bar for driving enjoyment.

10. BMW 3-Series

BMW's 3-Series represented a new choice for the consumer. The German manufacturer released its E90 3-Series in mid-2005 and it quickly became its bestselling car, particularly in the United States. Available in saloon, coupé, convertible and estate versions, the 3-Series delivered a luxury driving experience backed up by German engineering. The M3 topped off the class, powered by a V8 engine, producing 450bhp. In 2009, the E90 was given a major overhaul with the main external changes being a new bonnet, which gave the car more character. Mercedes and Audi now had to respond to BMW.

• STATS AND FACTS •

STILL GOING STRONG
The current generation of the 3 Series is the sixth Incarnation of BMW's classic executive saloon and is more popular than ever.

TURNED OFF
The E90 3-Series featured Efficient Dynamics, which amongst other things automatically stops the engine when the car is stationary.

Minis and Superminis

By the beginning of 2000, the supermini occupied four of the top ten places in the UK bestseller list and the 2000s would see its popularity increase further. Traditional favourites, such as the Fiesta, would continue to sell well, Peugeot would produce its first small car for more than a decade and another old favourite would return.

The beginning of the 21st century saw the experienced Fiesta still going strong and leading the way in the supermini sector. The Fiesta was now 25 years old and in 2002 the sixth generation, known as the **MkVI**, was unleashed. The new model featured rebadged Duratec engines and updated the exterior shape to cope with the aesthetic demands of the new century. Extras such as ABS and passenger airbags were now offered as standard, all of which helped the MkVI to become the bestselling Fiesta so far.

The Fiesta was fun to drive, as this advertising shot conveyed very clearly. This was the MkVI.

2005 saw the MkVI given a facelift, which brought some minor cosmetic changes to the exterior. Internally, the fascias were given a softer feel and options such as power-folding wing mirrors, automatic wipers and Bluetooth technology were added to the range. These changes had a startling effect on the ageing Fiesta, increasing sales by 25 per cent within a year and ensuring that Ford would keep the car in production for some time to come. In 2008, the model was changed again and the **MkVII** added features such as steering wheel controls for the stereo and keyless entry. Throughout the 2000s, Ford was careful not to neglect the Fiesta's roots and released versions of the sporty **Fiesta ST** with every new generation. The Fiesta was still a force to be reckoned with, but other manufacturers were queuing up to take its crown.

The MkVII Fiesta moved the supermini game on yet again.

Peugeot had famously missed out on the supermini revolution when it had decided not to produce a successor to the bestselling 205. In 1998, the French company rectified the error and added the **206** to its range. It was a wise move and by 2010 the 206 had become Peugeot's bestselling car, ever. Indeed, it was the bestselling car in Europe between 2001 and 2003 and today it is a popular car on the forecourts of second-hand dealers, as it's always sought after. The success of the 206 made a follow up inevitable and, in 2006, the **207** was launched. Available with a range of petrol and diesel engines, the 207 was also available in an estate and coupé-cabrio format. A GT and GTi variant came along at the same time, utilising a turbocharged 1.6-litre engine that could produce a more than respectable 150bhp, ensuring that the 207 could compete with the Fiesta ST.

The 206 and the 207 sold well but they, along with the other cars in the class, suffered

'Failure is simply the opportunity to start again, this time more intelligently'
Henry Ford

The MkVI Fiesta was offered in sporty ST guise; it was fast, but discreet at the same time.

The three-door Peugeot 206 was stylish; it sold alongside estate, five-door hatch and coupé-cabrio versions.

due to the rebirth of a truly classic small car. BMW had bought the Rover Group, in 1994, and had thereby acquired the Mini marque. When Rover was broken up in 2000, the German company was careful to keep the Mini brand for itself; it had plans to revolutionise the supermini market by bringing back the British classic.

The **MINI One**, the basic version of the new Mini, was tasked with taking the first bold steps into the modern supermini market, and it represented quite a risk for BMW.

Peugeot had missed out on the supermini revolution

The original Mini was a classic that was loved dearly by those who drove it and it was unique when compared with other small cars of its time. The new version of the Mini would be far more in line with the cars of the new century and it was far from assured that it would be a success. The MINI One kept the essential shape of the original, but it was considerably larger than its ancestor. It was also far more refined, embracing modernity and the comforts of the 21st century small car. The One was an instant success and **Cooper** and **Cooper S** versions soon followed. Again, this was essential if the new MINI was really to take hold in the marketplace and both variants were designed to take a range of Cooper Works add-ons and tuning updates from the off. The engine size across the range was a healthy 1.6 litres and on the Cooper S that was backed up with a supercharger, ensuring that the little car packed plenty of punch; a scooped bonnet added flair and distinction to the S model, too.

Later in its life, a whole series of special edition Peugeot 206s were released.

Seen here are the Peugeot 207CC (coupé-cabrio), three-door hatch and five-door estate.

Within five years the MINI's ascent was becoming momentous. In 2005, a convertible version was released and it featured a fully automatic roof, similar to the one pioneered in the Z4, which also featured a heated glass rear window. The range had become a big seller for BMW and, in 2007, the necessary second generation was brought to the market.

The MkII incorporated new engines and a revised exterior style. Every panel was changed from the earlier version and the overall length was slightly increased. The success of the MINI One had given BMW the confidence to make the MkII bigger and this enabled legroom to be slightly increased. An engine start button was also added, giving the car a sporty feel. The second generation saw the birth of a multitude of MINI variants. In 2008 the **MINI Clubman** was introduced; the estate version of the car. It featured an easy access door on the side and the MINI was now quite literally anything but mini.

MINIS / SUPERMINIS OF THE 2000S

1. Ford Fiesta MkVI
2. Ford Fiesta MkVII
3. Peugeot 206
4. Peugeot 207
5. MINI One
6. MINI Cooper
7. MINI Clubman

Many wondered if BMW had gone too far with the MINI Coupé; a car that looked awkward and was impractical.

Within five years the MINI's ascent was becoming momentous

BMW was keen to highlight the MINI's Britishness; all examples are built in the UK.

BMW decided to use the Clubman badge as it lent credibility to the new car, but it was also because it hadn't initially owned the traditional Traveller and Countryman badges, which had been previously used on the estate versions of the original car. Hot on the heels of the Clubman, in 2009, was the new convertible and a limited edition John Cooper Works model was also unveiled in the same year. An electric version, the MINI E, a MINI SUV, known as the Countryman, and even a MINI Coupé soon followed suit, showing that BMW had finally made the Mini brand its own. In 2009, the MINI was the seventh bestselling car in Britain and few would bet against BMW improving on this over the coming years.

It was the MINI that really defined the supermini market during the 2000s. It may have been a brave decision, but it was one that paid off and as the future beckons the competition may have to think again if they are going to be able to compete with the reborn legend that is the mighty MINI.

There was never an open-topped version available of the original Mini, but BMW introduced the MINI Convertible in 2005.

The facelifted first-generation Focus looked even smarter than the original edition.

Small Family Cars

At the end of the decade Ford was at the top of the bestseller lists, once again. In the Focus, Ford had another world-beating car, but Vauxhall would fiercely compete for the best small car of the 2000s. The Golf finally got the credit it deserved and Skoda became a serious option.

Over the past 50 years Ford has had its critics. Often the cars the 'men from America' built were accused of being cheap, or badly put together, or uninspired. Ford's reaction was usually to take note of the criticism, make the changes and improve on the product. It also had the ability to look to the future, buck styling trends and anticipate the ebb and flow of the market. With these things in mind, it's fair to say that in the Focus, Ford created one of the best small family cars of all time.

The **MkI Focus** was an immediate hit and there was very little that could be said against it. In 2004, with the second generation, Ford ironed out any minor issues there were and sales figures continued to rise. The excellent suspension was kept and the bodyshell was slightly stiffened, in an attempt to improve on the already impressive handling. There was also a **MkII** ST, available from 2005, which could achieve 0–60 in less than six and a half seconds, thanks to an engine that produced 222bhp.

In 2008, the **MkIII Focus** improved again on the MkII. Exterior changes such as a new bonnet and sculpted headlights gave the Focus a facelift and, to top it all off, it also managed to improve on the impressive MkIII ST.

The hottest production hatch so far; the Focus RS MkII.

Ford had the ability to look to the future and buck styling trends

The Ford Focus RS MkII could top 160mph; incredible for a relatively small family car.

It didn't matter that the RS series was beyond the pocket of the average family man

But, anyone who had bought a new ST in 2008 would have been crying into their bucket seats in 2009, when the awesome RS MkII was unveiled. The car packed a 2.5-litre 5-cylinder Turbo Volvo engine that produced a shatteringly powerful 301bhp – it had a top speed of 164mph! Ironically, while the proud owners of the new Focus RS MkII were laughing at the poor ST drivers, in the rear view mirror they would have seen something to wipe the smile from their face.

Before the decade was out Ford had released a strictly limited edition Focus RS500 – only 500 of which were ever made. The RS500 was only available in black; even the wheels were black. The engine was staggeringly powerful, emitting 351bhp, which added 3mph to the RS MkII's top speed and shaved its 0–60 time by 0.3 seconds. From the 500 that were built, 106 were sold to customers in the UK. And this was part of the secret of Ford's success. With the Focus it produced a small family car that was the top of its class. Every generation improved on the last and, for the new car buyer, there was no real reason to look at the alternatives.

But prospective Ford customers could be put off by the old criticisms about uninspired and dodgy workmanship. Models like the ST and RS series countered this problem by offering people a memory of cars like the Fiesta XR2, or the XR3i. The target

The fifth-generation Vauxhall Astra was better than ever, but it still looked a little bland.

When the fifth-generation Golf was launched, it would have been unthinkable for there not to be a GTi edition.

market for the Focus was people with families, who quite possibly used to own one of these old classics, in their younger days, and if they didn't, they probably wanted to. It didn't matter that the RS series was beyond the pocket of the average family man – when he bought the mid-range model he could imagine he was in a world-beater, and in all honesty, he was.

Vauxhall ensured that the Focus had some competition by completely revamping the venerable Astra. The **Astra MkV** was on the forecourts in the early part of 2004 and it was a very different car from its predecessor. Everything, both inside and out, was changed and the car was a big hit with buyers; with whom it didn't seem to matter that much of the motoring press found the MkV fairly uninspiring.

Volkswagen's Golf finally managed to produce a decent showing during the 2000s. The car had long been admired by the motoring press and the public, and was often seen as being on a level slightly above that of Vauxhall and Ford. But the price tag had always stopped it from becoming a really big seller.

While the Golf MkV was a brilliant car, VW surpassed itself with the creation of the MkVI.

The original Octavia allowed Skoda to turn a corner and leave its past behind, although some potential buyers were still unsure.

In 2009, the **MkVI Golf** began to change that. Volkswagen claimed that the car was cheaper to produce than the previous MkV and that these savings would be passed on to the customer, bringing the price down, if not by very much. The car dealt with the minor problems of the MkV by improving the interior trim and spec, and updating the diesel engines. By 2009, the Golf was 35 years old and had impressive sales figures for a car that was always said to be too expensive. Almost 1.5 million had been sold in Britain since its inception, making it amongst the top ten most popular cars ever sold in the UK.

Skoda may have been the butt of all car jokes since the days of the Iron Curtain, but it underwent a revival during the 2000s. The **MkI Octavia**, released in 1996, proved to be reliable and well built, but still suffered from the stigma of its past. In 2004, the **MkII** was released and the car shared the same basic platform as the Audi A3, MkV Golf and SEAT Leon, giving it credibility from the off. Slowly but surely the Octavia managed to change the public's mind about Skoda. In 2006, *Top Gear* voted it a 'masterpiece of dependability' and

SMALL FAMILY CARS OF THE 2000S

1. Ford Focus MkI, II & III
2. Vauxhall Astra MkV
3. Volkswagen Golf MkVI
4. Skoda Octavia MkI & II

The second generation Octavia built on the success of the first and became one of the best cars in its class.

Auto Express claimed it was the 'most satisfying car to own, in 2007'. This was praise indeed and while the Octavia may not challenge the supremacy of the Focus, it is now a force to be reckoned with and has earned the right, through reliability and build-quality, to be mentioned in the same breath as its more recognised peers. Quite an achievement.

As well as a five-door hatch, the MkII Octavia could also be bought in estate form.

'The Octavia was the most satisfying car to own, in 2007'

Auto Express

As the 2000s drew to a close it was hard to imagine the Focus being surpassed, at least in the foreseeable future. Vauxhall offered the most likely competition, but they would have to consider changing the Astra brand, as it was now becoming dated, if they wanted to lead rather than follow. Volkswagen and Skoda were steadily improving and they both continued to rise up the best selling lists, but they had a long way to go to reach the heights of the marvellous Ford Focus.

The third-generation Mondeo was bigger and better than ever, but that Ford badge deterred buyers.

Large Family Cars

The large family car sector may not have been as popular as in the heady days of the Cortina, but there was still space in the showrooms for a larger car. Ford's Mondeo would continue to impress and so too would Vauxhall's offerings. There would also be strong showings from Volkswagen and Toyota.

At the turn of the century the future looked bleak for the large family car. The trend had been heading towards the smaller end of the market for quite some time and the advent of the MPV had largely made the big car redundant. The prescribed audience had dissipated to such an extent that by the end of the decade the Mondeo, the bestselling traditional family car, was down at number nine in the country's top ten best-seller list. This fall from grace was further highlighted when the respected *Parker's Car Guide* published a feature, in December 2010, entitled 'Top Ten Family Car Bargains', which listed seven of the top ten as being MPVs.

For those in the market for a large car there were choices from Audi and BMW

Audi pretty much started the compact executive hatchback class, with its A3 and high-performance S3.

For those in the market for a large car there were upmarket choices from **Audi**, in the form of the **A3** and **A4**, and **BMW** in the shape of the **3 and 5-Series ranges**. These cars now represented their own vehicle class, often referred to as the compact executive, again showing how much the large car had fallen out of favour with the public. The German manufacturers also offered their SUV ranges, all of which were selling well and were more affordable than ever before. For the more

Alongside the BMW 3-Series, the Audi A4 has become the default choice for company car drivers in the UK.

The fifth-generation 3-Series was offered in M3 form; this is one of the rare saloon editions.

modest budget the MPV could offer style, space and economy, further diluting the pool of buyers.

Luckily, the larger car sector had always been the domain of the fleet car company and the travelling businessman, so there was still a job for the major manufacturers to do. Ford displayed its usual foresight when it revealed the **MkIII Mondeo** at the beginning of the decade. It was a new car for a new century and it did not disappoint. Ford had taken on board comments concerning the lack of rear passenger legroom and as the MkIII was larger than its predecessor, this helped to solve the issue. A new 2-litre diesel engine replaced the disappointing Endura turbodiesel and the Mondeo was generally improved all round.

Ford labelled the Mondeo 'one of the safest places to be'

Safety was one of the MkIII Mondeo's USPs and Ford employed a clever computer system that would automatically determine which airbags to employ in the case of a crash. It was entitled the 'Intelligent Protection System' and this, along with the addition of anti-lock brakes across the entire range, led Ford to label the Mondeo 'one of the safest places to be'. Rather disappointingly for Ford the car didn't fare as well as its rivals in the Euro NCAP safety tests. The Mondeo continues to dominate its sector, helping to ensure that the model was the bestselling car in its class throughout the decade, and continues to be so even today.

Vauxhall has long been successful in the large car arena. The Cavalier was an excellent product and the **Vectra** had also done well against the competition's offerings. In 2008, Vauxhall replaced the Vectra with the **Insignia**, which was unveiled at the British International Motor Show, in London. A year later it won the coveted European Car of the Year award and outsold the Mondeo. It was deserved; good design and clever technology had ensured that the car was well received.

The Insignia could match or even better the Mondeo on safety grounds. It embraced adaptive headlighting with multiple beam options, along with sensors controlling the car's running lights. There was also the option of an upmarket satellite navigation system, which utilised a small camera in the windscreen to keep watch for traffic signs. The electronics could also trigger an alert if the car veered out of its lane. The engine range offered value for money in the 1.6 and 1.8-litre variants and power in the 2.0 turbo and 2.8-litre V6 options. Six-speed gearboxes were also fitted as standard across the entire range. From launch, the Insignia looked more composed than the Mondeo and with a good level of trim it is not surprising that it has matched the Mondeo for sales.

It was over the course of the 1990s that Volkswagen's **Passat** first started to show potential and during the 2000s the release of the B6 model suggested that it was becoming a serious option to the traditional fare. The latest, and current, Passat was first seen

Ever since it first appeared the 5-Series has been the enthusiast driver's choice. This is the fifth-generation model.

The pre-facelift MkII Vectra was a missed opportunity for Vauxhall.

LARGE FAMILY CARS OF THE 2000S

1. Audi A3
2. Audi A4
3. BMW 3-Series
4. BMW 5-Series
5. Ford Mondeo MkIII
6. Vauxhall Vectra
7. Vauxhall Insignia
8. Volkswagen Passat
9. Toyota Avensis

at the Geneva Motor Show in 2006 and it closely matched the competition in terms of engines and interior specifications; the Passat shares much of the same technology utilised by Audi and clearly benefits as a result.

At the end of the decade a facelift improved the look of the Passat's rather tame front-end and added safety technology was also installed. A system of sensors in the car recognises changes in driver behaviour and alerts to possible dangers. There is also an emergency braking system available, further enhancing the Passat's safety credentials. Despite the quality of the Passat, Volkswagen also markets its own MPVs – the Touran and the Sharan – and these no doubt take sales away from the capable Passat.

Toyota was just one of a number of Japanese car makers that had been steadily making a name for themselves in the UK and in 2003 it released the MkII **Avensis** to general acclaim.

Toyota wanted to offer something different – a wise decision

The car was a welcome surprise and vastly improved on the MkI. Toyota wanted to offer something different – a wise move in the family sector, so it designed the car to be enjoyable to drive and have as much haptic involvement with the driver as possible. The Avensis also offered decent levels of engine choice and interior specification and became the first Japanese car to receive a five-star Euro NCAP score, proving its safety qualifications were up to date.

The Insignia finally gave Vauxhall a large family car that could compete on equal terms with the Mondeo.

All these cars were worthy options, it was just that they were playing to an audience that had already left the theatre. The reality was that over the last 50 years demand for the large family car had been in almost constant decline. By the start of the 21st century its time had almost passed. It remains to be seen if the Mondeo or Insignia can maintain their status over the coming years.

The original Toyota Avensis was criticised for being impossibly bland, but at least it was extremely reliable.

The BMW 7-Series has long represented a slightly left-field choice for the wealthy wanting discreet luxury transport.

Luxury Cars

The start of the 2000s brought with it a new selection of top marque cars from the likes of Rolls-Royce and Maybach, and the German manufacturers now sat in pole position. However, the financial sector meltdown, which occurred during the first decade of the century, meant that the luxury car market experienced a downturn in sales.

The luxury car market has always relied on 'the good times' in order to survive and prosper. There will always be a market for these cars as the people associated with 'old money' are not so affected by the ups and downs of the financial markets. But, since the boom of the 1980s, there have been a lot more people in the market for the very best vehicles in the world. The ranks of the rich have been swelled through the growth of the banking industry in the UK and the rampant and, some would argue, completely unchecked march of capitalism. This provided a much bigger target market for the luxury car maker, and as a result more models became available in the market and more money was ploughed into research and development, in order to create the dream cars of tomorrow.

During the 2000s the dream cars of tomorrow were available today and the market saw the emergence of some truly breathtaking cars. But the problem was that the anticipated market was no longer there. The financial crash of the mid-to-late 2000s had not only destroyed the fortunes of many, but had persuaded many others to be more conservative with their money. A nice BMW 7-Series became preferable to a Bentley. While Britain and the West have been experiencing these problems, the growing markets of Russia, China and India have ensured that the luxury car makers have stayed in business, so for the time being at least, the future looks rosy for the super-rich.

During the 2000s the dream cars of tomorrow were available today

One of the most impressive car makers of the last hundred years is the German manufacturer, Maybach. Today Daimler owns the company but unfortunately, it has suffered due to the financial crisis which is why Maybach will soon be closed down. Even so, the company's final offerings – the

When the Chris Bangle-designed fourth-generation 7-Series appeared, it was criticised for its clumsy lines.

Maybach 57 and **62** – have risen to the very top of the luxury car list. The cars are based on a concept car that was shown at the 1997 Tokyo Motor Show. In 2008, the Luxury Brand Index voted Maybach as the number one luxury car maker in the world, and with good reason.

The Maybach 57S carries a 6-litre Mercedes-Benz engine that can hurl the huge car to 60mph in less than 5 seconds. On top of this performance the car boasts exquisite luxury. Standard features include a voice recognition navigation system, DVD players, heated seats that also massage their occupants, top quality leather upholstery, night vision, rear-view camera and a heated steering wheel. On top of the standard features there are a host of options that include additions such as a voice-activated sunroof. The cost of the 57S in Europe is currently just under €370,000.

The 62S is the 57's bigger brother and incorporates all of the 57's features and a host of others, such as folding tables in the back

The Maybach 57 and 62 have risen to the very top of the luxury car list

It's huge – and hugely expensive – but the Maybach is little more than a stretched Mercedes S-Class. Which is why buyers shunned it.

In Europe and North America the Maybach is seen as rather too flash, but it suits perfectly the tastes of those in the Middle East.

and an optional panoramic sunroof. There is also the option of a communication system that allows the occupants to communicate with people outside the car, without even opening the windows. The 62S is available at a cost of €493,000. Both versions are also available as a limited edition 'Zeppelin' variant which incorporates larger engines and even finer quality leather upholstery.

Not to be outdone, in 2003 Rolls-Royce revealed the **Phantom**, which could match the Maybach pound for pound. Rolls-Royce, like Maybach, is owned by a German company, in this case BMW, and the Phantom was the first Rolls-Royce to be produced under BMW's ownership. The Phantom has similar performance ability to the Maybach with a claimed 0–60 time of 5.7 seconds and comes with all the luxury anyone can want. There are 44,000 paint colours on offer, the doors are remote control, rear-view cameras aid parking and the Phantom carries the ultimate in sound systems. There is also a built-in fridge, and even the famous Spirit of Ecstasy ornament retracts into the car when it's parked so that it can't be stolen. Rolls-Royce claim that it will add any option to the car that a customer requires. On release, the Phantom's basic price was £250,000.

Away from these super-luxury cars there are also plenty of options for the more modestly rich banker or hedge fund manager. 2009 saw BMW release the latest version of the luxury **7-Series**. The 740 models are capable of producing 326bhp, which sends the BMW to 60mph in just 6 seconds and the 750i is capable of reaching the same speed in just 5.2 seconds. Inside, the car is decked out with

The Phantom is a massive car, with a price tag to match.

A Roller is still the car of choice for the discerning Englishman

the expected wood and leather and it features a standard navigation system screen that is 10 inches wide. TV screens are fitted into the back of the front-seat headrests and each rear passenger can choose independently what they watch. The 7-Series also sports front, rear and side-view cameras – similar to the ones in the Rolls-Royce Phantom – which are capable of individual pedestrian recognition, night vision and issuing lane change warnings.

A new Mercedes-Benz **S-Class** is due in 2012, but the current top-end Benz is still seriously impressive. Mercedes refers to it as the 'best car in the world' and although it's bound to say that, it has a good claim to the title. There are bigger engined S-Classes, but the performance of the 350 CDI is outstanding and at a starting cost of £56,000 it provides good value for money. 60mph is achieved in a little over 8 seconds and the top speed is 146mph. The diesel engine will also allow for an economical 35.8 mpg, meaning that savings can be made on fuel, allowing more to be spent on the optional extras.

Not to be outdone by its German rivals, Lexus continued to build on the success of the LS400 when in 2000 they released the third generation **LS430**. The standard suspension from the previous model was replaced and the whole car was redesigned to be more conspicuous. Inside, on top of the usual refinery, the LS430 featured exquisite walnut trim on the dashboard and doors, as well as a voice-recognition controlled navigation

The Phantom is impressively engineered; even the wheel centre caps are designed to stay upright as the car moves along.

Ever since it first went on sale, the Mercedes S-Class has represented the very pinnacle of passenger car development.

system and touch-screen centre console. The car was further improved in 2003 when the range was given a facelift, which included a revised exterior styling and even more interior extras.

The luxury car market may have suffered slightly during the late 2000s, but as long as there is wealth there will be luxury cars. Maybach may be coming to an end, but their cars are amongst the most luxurious ever produced. A Roller is still the car of choice for the discerning Englishman, but BMW and Mercedes are now becoming a popular luxury car of choice, offering top-notch refinement for a reasonable price, in a car that doesn't look like you've just been to tea with the Queen.

Options for the LS430 included heated and cooled front seats, power sunshade, a fridge, and air purifier.

LUXURY CARS OF THE 2000S

1. Maybach 57S / 62S
2. Rolls-Royce Phantom
3. BMW 7-Series
4. Mercedes S-Class
5. Lexus LS430

Congestion charging given the green light

The car had experienced such a meteoric rise over the last 50 years that by the start of the 2000s there were unprecedented numbers of them on the roads of Britain. The country's ageing road network began to struggle under the sheer weight of numbers and the congestion in some parts of the country was practically unbearable. London was worse than anywhere else and in the year 2000 the average speed realistically obtainable in the capital city was about 10mph, the same as it had been a hundred years before.

Change is on the way

It was in 1973 that people first started to pay attention to the environmental impact the rising number of cars was having. Once again, the public showed its power and this weight of opinion began to influence car designers. Over the proceeding decades, environmental issues continued to take centre stage in society, politics and car design, as concerns continued to grow over the levels of CO2 that millions of exhaust pipes were belching out, every day.

As a result, over the last 30 years, cars have become considerably cleaner. But, despite the decreasing levels of pollution, simply leaving things to the car designers was not going to suffice and the country's politicians would have to get involved if immediate change was going to happen. By the end of 2002, the pollution problem in London had become a serious issue.

Top: Ken Livingstone gave London congestion charging.
Centre: The charge was meant to cut congestion in the capital.
Bottom: Originally, only central London was covered by the charge.

Congestion charging

Something had to be done and in February 2003 a controversial congestion charge was introduced for drivers travelling through the city centre. The charge was levied at £5 per day (but has since risen to £10), which was considered enough to deter casual motorists, but also be affordable for those needing to drive into the city centre. The charge applied between the hours of 0700 and 1800 and severe fines were imposed on those who declined, or forgot, to pay.

Records show that on the first day approximately 190,000 vehicles passed through the restricted zone, which was about 25 per cent less than the usual number. However, it should be noted that this day coincided with the school half term, so traffic was always going to be less than normal. The implementation of the congestion charge required a sizeable investment and it was therefore imperative that it showed results. In 2007, Transport for London declared that there had been a consistent 16 per cent reduction in vehicle numbers traversing the centre of the city, and that the system was improving the general flow of traffic. It was also generating hundreds of millions of pounds a year for TFL.

The congestion charge continues to be controversial and at the end of 2011, Boris Johnson, the incumbent Mayor of London, withdrew the western extension to the zone, which had been implemented in 2007 by the previous mayor, Ken Livingstone. While the charge initially reduced traffic levels in central London, it didn't take long for congestion to get back to the pre 2003 level. However, this is not to say that congestion charging is a failure. Traffic may have risen but it was bound to as cars became more accessible. Pollution is an issue that must be tackled and although London may have been the first city to take action, it certainly won't be the last.

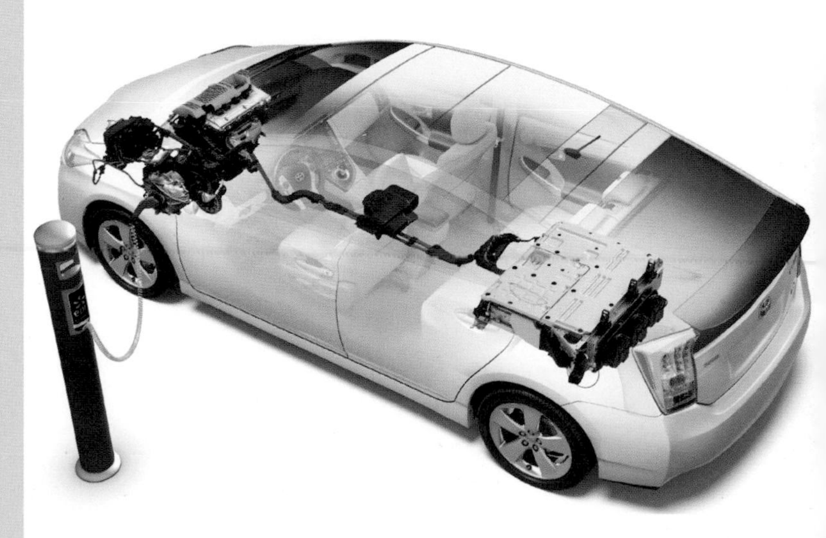

Top: The original Prius was congestion charge exempt.
Centre: Electric cars are seen as an answer to pollution.
Bottom: The latest Prius can be recharged from the mains.

The Bugatti Veyron SuperSport is currently the world's fastest production car, capable of an incredible 268mph.

Sports Cars

Over the preceding decades, car manufacturers had been steadily amalgamating in order to save money and pool resources. In the 1980s, Ford had bought Jaguar and Aston Martin, and Volvo soon followed. In 1998 Daimler-Benz and the Chrysler Corporation joined forces to create DaimlerChrysler. The Volkswagen-Audi partnership acquired Lamborghini, Bentley and the remains of Bugatti. BMW bought the Mini brand, and Ferrari, which was still part of Fiat in the late 1960s, had achieved enough solo success to take over Maserati.

The long-term aims of this series of amalgamations were to reach fruition in the 2000s, with the creation of some world-beating supercars and generation-defining production cars. Over the decade cars like the Ferrari Enzo, Lamborghini Murcielago, Pagani Zonda S, Koenigsegg CC and the magnificent

The 'noughties' gave us the first million-pound supercar, the resurrection of a legend and the ability to go from 0–60 in under three seconds. The sports car now occupied a large percentage of the garage forecourt, and companies such as BMW, Mazda and Volkswagen would take full advantage of the public's love affair with speed.

Bugatti Veyron would light up the sports car world, achieving heights that only a decade before had been unthinkable. There would also be notable production cars such as the new BMW MINI Cooper S, the BMW Z4, the Nissan 350Z and the Honda S2000. Plus, of course, there were to be refinements to existing models such as Volkswagen's Golf GTi, BMW's M3 and Mazda's MX-5, all of which would go from strength to strength.

The Ferrari Enzo was a shatteringly fast track-ready road car.

In 2002, Ferrari compounded the success of the F40 and F50 with the release of the **Enzo**, which expressed the very latest in Formula 1 technology. Only 400 Enzos were ever built, but the car is undoubtedly one of the finest models Ferrari has ever produced. It featured advanced composite bodywork along with a carbon-fibre and aluminium honeycomb chassis, enabling it to hold the road with grace and precision. Under the bonnet the Enzo packed a 6-litre V12, which produced a spine-tingling 660bhp, hurling the Ferrari to 217mph. The car boasted extremely advanced aerodynamics that had cascaded down from Ferrari's Formula 1 machines, creating enough downforce to stop the car literally taking off under its extreme acceleration, which could send the Enzo to 60mph from standstill in 3.5 seconds. This style and performance came at a cost. The cost of a new Enzo was £450,000, but should you want a second-hand model today, the cost would be nearer to £700,000.

Lamborghini's V12 two-seaters have always been dramatic; this is the Murcielago.

The price of the Ferrari Enzo, at launch, was £450,000

When the Murcielago was driven at speed, those vents above the rear wheels opened up to allow more air in to cool the engine.

The Aston Martin Vanquish was beautiful, but at the same time very aggressive.

In 1997, it looked like Lamborghini may have been living on borrowed time. The cash-strapped company simply didn't have the funds to compete in the upper echelons of the supercar market. However, in 1998 Volkswagen rode to the rescue, buying the legendary car maker and thereby making possible the development of one of Lamborghini's finest ever cars; the **Murcielago**. The car was named after a remarkable bull that, in 1879, took 24 sword thrusts during a fight and, against all odds, survived. The Murcielago was aptly named, for it oozed power, stature and strength. Replacing the Diablo, the Murcielago was produced by Lamborghini until 2010, ensuring that Lamborghini could compete with the supercars of Ferrari, Porsche and Bugatti.

The Murcielago had a top speed of 205mph and a 0–60 time of just 3.8 seconds. But the car was not just about its bullish power; it was beautifully designed and featured the

The Vanquish would make its mark in the James Bond film *Die Another Day*.

Porsche continued to develop its iconic 911; this generation is known as the 997.

same scissor doors made so famous by the Countach. When Volkswagen acquired Lamborghini the design for the Murcielago was reworked several times. The car had to be perfect to compete and ultimately the Belgian designer, Luc Donckerwolke, was chosen. It was his creation and Volkswagen's money that together saved the famous manufacturer from obscurity.

'The Bugatti Veyron is a complete piece of junk'

Ron Dennis, Executive Chairman of McLaren Automotive

The Enzo and Murcielago were by no means the only supercars of the noughties. Porsche released its **911 GT2** and Carrera GT, Aston Martin gave us the **Vanquish** and Audi produced the wonderful R8. Pagani and **Koenigsegg** also produced notable cars, but there was another machine that was to outshine them all; the **Bugatti Veyron EB 16.4**.

The Veyron is the fastest road car ever built and even the original version was capable of achieving speeds in excess of 250mph. It was first shown to the world at the Paris Motor Show in 2000 and at the

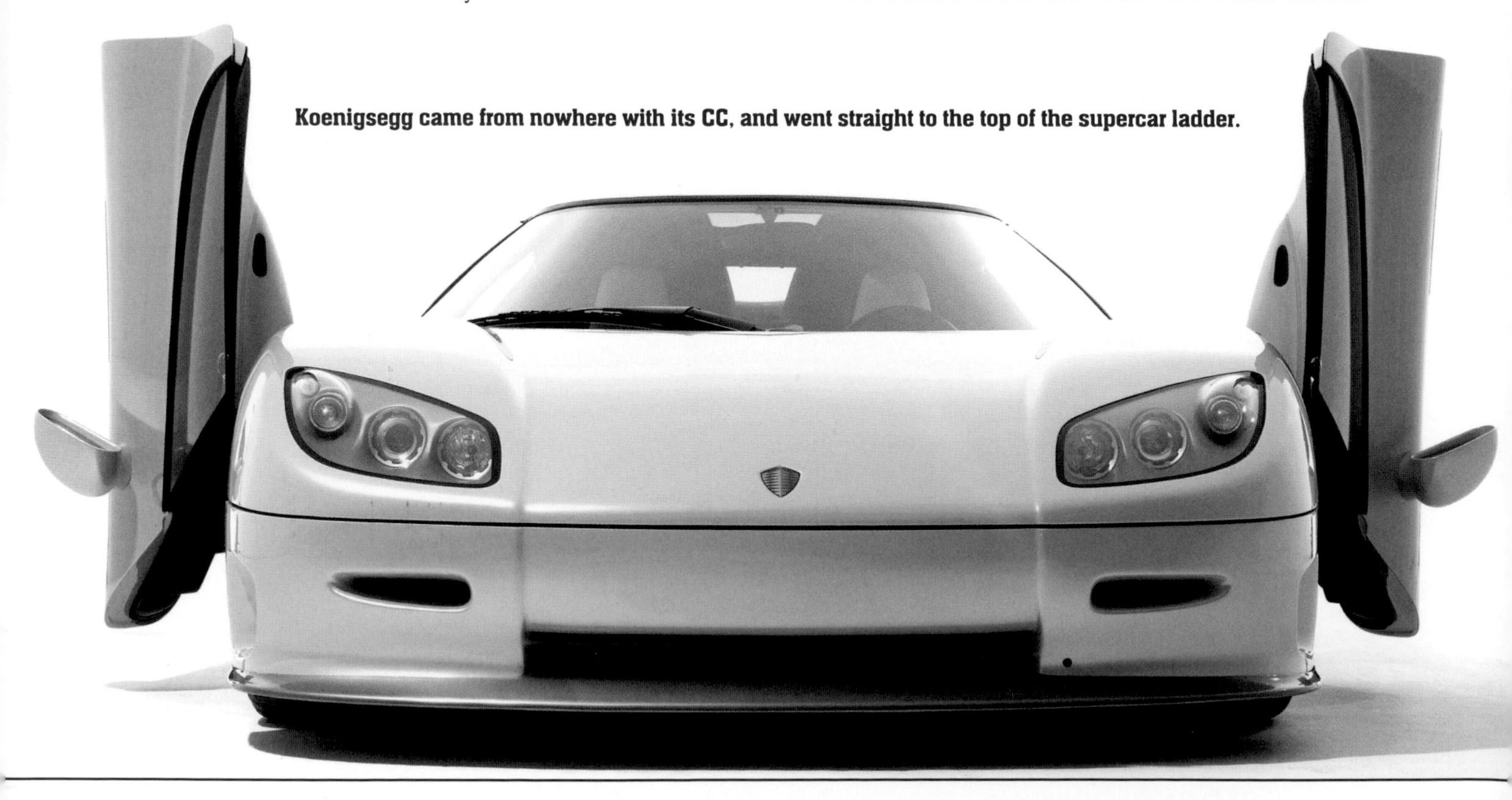

Koenigsegg came from nowhere with its CC, and went straight to the top of the supercar ladder.

The Bugatti Veyron is a remarkable car, with its quad-turbo 8-litre 16-cylinder engine.

time it was still a concept car, but today it is on its third incarnation, all of which have steadily improved on the original. The Veyron produced a scarcely believable 987bhp, from a revolutionary 8-litre, 16-cylinder, quad-turbo engine that achieved 0–60mph in a staggering 2.4 seconds. In 2010, the Super Sport version of this majestical car managed a top speed of 268mph, a speed that may never be equalled again. The Veyron is a demonstration of what is possible in car manufacture and design, but the investment required to create its equal is unlikely to be found any time soon. Bugatti sold fewer than 300 Veyrons, but it did have a price tag of over £1m.

Away from the world of the supercars there were many notable sports cars released during the noughties. Porsche's **Boxster S** debuted in 2000 and its success lead to a further generation, in 2005. Fast and stylish, it was a cheaper alternative to the 911.

The Boxster S was smaller than the 911, but still embodied the Porsche ethos.

The original BMW Z4 was wonderful to drive and a marked improvement on the Z3.

Launched in 2001, the new BMW MINI was an immediate success. Larger than the original car, the new model was equipped to deal with a world that had moved on from the 1960s. But it was in 2002 that the new MINI truly rediscovered its sporting roots, when the release of the Cooper S version consolidated the reputation of the new car. Producing 170bhp, the supercharged **Cooper S** was capable of a respectable 140mph and a 0–60 time of less than 7 seconds. A new Mini may have been a risk, but BMW did not disappoint.

BMW also used the noughties to upgrade its ageing Z3. The **Z4** was a traditional roadster, for a new century. The 3-litre version was capable of an electronically limited 155mph and flew to 60mph in 5.7 seconds. The Z4 was an affordable car that delivered far more than its price tag suggested. It needed to, as there was stiff competition from Audi's updated TT, **Nissan's 350Z** and the **Honda S2000**. With Volkswagen's improved GTi and BMW's M3 also in the marketplace, the consumer was spoiled for choice.

Technological developments, and the investment that was only possible from the refined and amalgamated car manufacturers, accelerated the sports car's development

The 3-litre version was capable of an electronicaly limited 155mph

The 350Z marked a return to form for Nissan; here it's seen in ultra-rare roadster guise.

throughout the decade. The Veyron, Murcielago and Enzo may have been the absolute pinnacle of driving, but, in one way, it was cars like the new MINI Cooper S and Z4 that allowed the average person to experience a driving experience that was far beyond reach only a few years before. As the 2000s ended sports cars were no longer just for the rich and famous. They were now available to everyone. Driving had become fun again and, just as in the 1960s, the thrill of the sports car was back. Let's hope it's here to stay.

The Honda S2000 stayed in production for a decade; it was one of the greatest driver's cars of the noughties.

SPORTS CARS OF THE 2000S

1. Ferrari Enzo
2. Lamborghini Murcielago
3. Porsche 911 GT2
4. Aston Martin Vanquish
5. Koenigsegg
6. Bugatti Veyron EB 16.4
7. Porsche Boxster S
8. MINI Cooper S
9. BMW Z4
10. Nissan 350Z
11. Honda S2000

As soon as it was introduced, the Range Rover Sport became a hit with buyers.

SUVs

The 1990s had seen the SUV become ever more prominent and it had begun to eclipse traditional ideas of a large family car. During the 2000s, the SUV would be further refined, creating more choice for the consumer, but also raising concerns over the place these vehicles have on the modern road.

Range Rover and Land Rover had blazed a trail during the 1990s and by the year 2000 other manufacturers were keen to follow suit. The Land Rover Discovery and the Range Rover had been fairly sparse in terms of luxury, but during the 2000s the more premium companies would go to great lengths to improve the spec of their ranges and entice more people to buy SUVs over the more traditional choice of larger family cars.

After the success of the Range Rover HSE, the company was keen to further refine the Range Rover and take it from being an eminently capable 4x4 to a premium car. One of the biggest advances was the development of the **Range Rover Sport**, which came to the market in 2005. The Sport is smaller than the traditional Range Rover and styled to mix a blend of 4x4 vehicle and executive car to create a new type of executive SUV. The Sport was designed to fit in between the Range Rover Vogue and the BMW 5-Series, in terms of car class. On release, the Sport cost between £36,000 and £57,500, depending on the spec, and this price enabled the Sport to really compete for attention.

> The Sport was designed to sit between the Vogue and the BMW 5-Series

Inside, the new model was roomy and the boot was still a decent size. The passenger cabin was more austere than the premium quality Range Rovers, but the price reflected this and there was still a lot for the money. Wood and leather were largely replaced with plastic, but plastic that didn't have a cheap feel. The seats gave a sporty feel and items like satellite navigation and leather upholstery were still available as add-ons.

Even though the Range Rover Sport was superb on-road, it could tackle rough terrain with equal aplomb.

The BMW X5 was the first full-size SUV to drive much like a regular road car. The Porsche Cayenne, seen here, was even better.

Under the bonnet, the Range Rover offered engine choices including the 2.7-litre V6 turbodiesel and the 4.2-litre supercharged petrol V8, which produced 390bhp. The 4.2-litre could power the Sport to 60mph in just over 7 seconds, but this performance came at a cost. The official fuel performance figures of 17.8mpg were not easy to obtain and on the motorway, at high speeds, the fuel consumption could easily be half that. Initial reviews of the Sport were positive and the Range Rover brand was able to add credibility to the Sport, as it was also a competent 4x4. Range Rover had history in this regard and this has helped the Sport to fare well against the younger pretenders, such as BMW and Porsche.

Porsche entered the SUV market in 2002. **The Cayenne** didn't take long to prove that it had the right stuff and reviews praised its handling and ride characteristics. The basic model utilised the same engine found in the Volkswagen Golf R32 and could take the Cayenne from 0–60 in 7.5 seconds. An S version was also available from launch, which was even quicker, shaving almost half a second off the 0–60 time. In 2006, a Turbo S version was unleashed and was aimed at competing with the Mercedes ML 63 AMG. A twin-turbo 4.5-litre V8 could achieve a top speed of 171mph and reach 60mph from a standing start in just 5 seconds, which was more than fast enough for a car that size.

Official fuel performance figures of 17.8mpg were hard to obtain

Porsche was careful to ensure that the Cayenne could perform out in the wild, away from the claustrophobic streets of Kensington

Despite its size, the Cayenne was seriously quick and handled superbly.

Having been so successful with its X5, BMW next moved downmarket with the highly regarded X3.

and accordingly spent a great deal of time off-road testing the vehicle. The results bore fruit and the Cayenne proved to be a competent 4x4. It would also comfortably seat five passengers and was kitted out with everything one would expect, from leather upholstery to a large-screen satellite navigation system. The Cayenne proved to be a wise move for Porsche and it was further updated at the end of the decade. Waiting lists grew for the 2010 edition and considering that it is amongst the most expensive SUVs on the market, that says a lot about the quality of the car.

Another new entry into the SUV market during the 2000s came from Audi. The **Q7** went on sale in 2007 and it is one of the largest SUVs on the road. The Q7 has a

Porsche was careful to ensure that the Cayenne could perform in the wild

permanent four-wheel drive system, of the well-regarded quattro variety, but it was not built to be an off-roader. What it lacked in off-road capabilities it made up for in on-road performance. The 4.2-litre TDI had a top speed of 146mph and could reach 60mph in less than 6.5 seconds. Inside, the Q7 can seat seven adults and, as can be imagined from its immense size, there was plenty

The Audi Q7 was massive, but at least it could seat seven.

of storage room in the boot. The standard features included an eight-speaker stereo, air conditioning and a CD player. Prices started at £37,980, meaning it was well placed to compete and, as most owners of an SUV will never take it off road, the Q7 is certainly a more than worthwhile alternative to the Range Rover.

BMW released the **X5** in 1999 and over the 2000s it developed it further. In 2006, a second generation was made available and the new version improved on the rather boxy look of the original by softening the edges and improving the front end. The X5 was selling so well that in 2003 a smaller SUV was marketed as the **X3**. This move saw the SUV begin to compete with the upmarket small family car class, which may have interesting consequences for the future of family driving. The X3 is already offered in second-generation form; it's a big improvement over the original, which suffered from a poor ride and an expensive price tag.

The Audi Q7 was as brilliantly developed as you'd expect of any car wearing those four rings.

The first-generation BMW X5 was a dynamic masterpiece.

Mercedes also refined the **ML** range with the second generation, released in 2005 and further updated in 2009. The new version was bigger than the original, but also more

During the 2000s the SUV cemented its place in driving folklore

streamlined and the 63 AMG version could reach 60mph in just 4.8 seconds, making it a match for Porsche's Cayenne.

During the 2000s the SUV cemented its place in driving folklore but it wasn't without its detractors. The Q7 was criticised for being far too big and the question remains as to the usefulness of these cars. They are uneconomical, can cause a great deal of

The second-generation BMW X5 is even better than the first, and capable of carrying seven people.

The second-generation Mercedes ML-Class was a huge improvement on the model that came before.

damage to anything they hit and with traffic congestion worsening all the time, they seem to be at odds with the trend for smaller cars. Nevertheless they continue to be popular and they give their drivers a feeling of safety and style, something that has always fared well in the world of motoring.

The original Mercedes ML was not as successful as was hoped.

SUVS OF THE 2000S

1. Range Rover Sport
2. Porsche Cayenne
3. Audi Q7
4. BMW X5
5. BMW X3
6. Mercedes ML

MPVs

By the start of the 2000s, the MPV was the most popular choice for buyers looking for a larger family car. It began to monopolise the marketplace as more and more manufacturers released their own versions and, along with the SUV, it spelled the end for the traditional family car.

The Ford Focus C-Max brought driving enjoyment to the compact MPV segment.

The family car journey has always been notorious for those endless questions of 'are we there yet?' or complaints from the backseat of 'he's on my side'. Space, in other words, has always been at a premium. Bigger cars allowed for a more harmonious family driving experience, but were expensive to buy, uneconomic to run and difficult to park. With the MPV you could have it all. There was plenty of space for the children, the dogs, the shopping and the children's friends. MPVs utilise space by going upwards and not outwards. It was the same principle that was applied to housing in the 1950s and 60s and it made sense. Seating passengers a little higher up than was the norm had the added bonus of giving the impression of freedom, of not being stuck in exhaust-filled traffic jams and of being able to take in the surroundings.

The Galaxy was more of a minibus than a standard family car

The S-Max was almost as big as a Galaxy, but it was designed to be significantly more sporty.

So it's not difficult to see why the MPV had become so popular, so quickly. By the end of the 1990s, they had really taken hold in the UK market and Ford was keen to exploit the new automotive format further. The Galaxy had been around since 1995, but it was an early impression of an MPV and because it was fairly rough and ready it didn't fare particularly well. The Galaxy was more of a minibus than a family car and, in 2003, Ford sought to change all that with the introduction of the **Focus C-Max**.

Never before had a seven-seater MPV been so good to drive; the S-Max was a turning point in the development of the people-carrier.

The Touran looked fairly unremarkable, but buyers loved it because of that hallowed VW badge.

The Focus C-Max used the same C1 platform as the Focus MkII, yet because it was bigger, it could comfortably accommodate five adults, with space to spare. Engine sizes ranged from the basic Duratec 1.4-litre right up to the 2.0-litre Duratorq diesel model, offering something for everybody in terms of power and performance. A facelift arrived in 2006 and at the same time the 'Focus' moniker was dropped, creating a unique brand name for Ford's range of MPVs.

As a compact MPV, the Touran could accommodate up to seven, while also offering multiple seating configurations.

In the same year Ford also released the **S-Max**, which was aimed at the larger car market. It was still smaller than the Galaxy, but larger than the C-Max and it was intended to be something of a saloon/MPV hybrid. It was very well received and, in 2006, the S-Max won the European Car of the Year award, not least because of its ingenious folding seat system, which allowed for a dynamic use of the interior space. Three versions were released for the UK market; the Edge, Zetec and Titanium, which as the name suggests was the top of the range model. The S-Max embodied all of Ford's usual safety features, including the Intelligent Protection System, multiple airbags and several anti-skid and stability measures. Part of the S-Max's success is down to the way it drives. It handles much more like a car than an MPV and it looks rather like an oversized hatchback.

The handling and the looks certainly helped the S-Max to be a success, but looks aren't everything in the MPV world, as was proved by the success of the **Volkswagen Touran**. Released in 2003, the Touran joined the Sharan in VW's MPV range but it didn't have the look of other MPVs in its class, the design was a touch plain and uninspiring, but it still had a great deal to offer, and won the *What Car?* Car of the Year award, in 2005.

The 2-litre TDI Sport version, released in 2007, came with leather seats, electric windows, air-conditioning, and all the usual optional add-ons such as a touch-screen sat-nav (costing an extra £1,175) and even an automatic parking system. It handled like a hatchback and its 2-litre turbodiesel engine could shift it to 60mph in only 9 seconds, and comfortably reach a top speed of 133mph. The Touran received a five-star Euro NCAP score and came with a three-year warranty. Despite its rather plain demeanour, the Touran is very well built and one of the best MPVs around.

The S-Max embodied all of Ford's usual safety features

Renault had started the compact MPV era when it announced the **Scenic** back in 1996, and in 2009 the third generation was unveiled. It coincided with the release of a

Renault continued to develop its Scenic and Grand Scenic; this is the second-generation model.

> According to Euro NCAP, the Verso is the safest MPV on the road

larger version, known as the Grand Scenic, which was still technically a compact MPV, but could seat seven people. Both MPVs took over where their predecessors had left off and continued to sell well. Citroen followed suit with the **C4 Picasso**, the replacement for the stalwart Xsara Picasso. Like the Scenic, the C4 Picasso was available in two sizes, the larger model carrying the Grand C4 Picasso tag. While the Xsara Picasso had been well received, the new C4-based model was a huge leap forward in terms of versatility, quality and running costs. The design was also much more modern, just like the third-generation Renault Scenic's, with both cars featuring very large and wide windscreens to take advantage of their height and also to increase the feeling of space and freedom inside the cabin.

While Renault and Citroen consolidated their positions in the market, a new contender emerged, in 2009. **The Verso**, Toyota's MPV, like the Scenic and Picasso, was also available in five or seven-seat forms. According to Euro NCAP, it's the safest MPV on the road and it comes to the market backed up by Toyota's respected reliability record. With ten different Versos available, ranging from the basic 1.6 V-matic to the 7-door 2.2-litre D-CAT T Spirit, there really is something for everybody.

The C4 Picasso's large windscreen made the interior seem bigger than it was.

The second-generation Verso of 2009 looked more dynamic and was much better to drive than its predecessor.

And things are bound to get even better, as Toyota is likely to introduce a hybrid edition, featuring Toyota's award-winning Hybrid Synergy Drive.

By the end of the decade, the MPV had shown that it was likely to represent the future of the family car. It could now offer everything the modern family required and, with the prospect of hybrid versions not too far off, we can expect to see more of these multi-purpose vehicles on the roads, for some time to come.

The original Toyota Verso was well built, versatile and reliable, but had a very low profile.

MPVS OF THE 2000S

1. Ford Focus C-Max
2. Ford Focus S-Max
3. Volkswagen Touran
4. Renault Scenic
5. Citroen C4 Picasso
6. Toyota Verso

The Prius has become the world's bestselling hybrid; this is a second generation model.

Electric and Hybrid Cars

Modern technology and ever-rising concerns over the impact cars were having on the environment meant that the advent of hybrid and electric cars came as no real surprise. The real shock was how good they were and how far they had developed in such a short time.

For the last 50 years, cars have got steadily more affordable and ever more popular. So, it's not surprising that the damage they cause to the environment has become more apparent, and consequently, more of a concern. But green issues are not the only problems with the traditional car. The roots of the internal combustion engine can be traced back to China, in the 13th century. It is an old technology that has survived because it works, it is understood and, of course, because it is inextricably linked to oil.

But the future of the car surely lies away from the internal combustion engine. Fossil fuels are rapidly diminishing and even modern engines are not particularly efficient. But most importantly of all, petrol is only going to get more expensive, meaning that unless car manufacturers change their approach, fewer and fewer people will be able to afford to own and run a car in the future. With vast swathes of the world still developing there is a massive potential market out there, and one that the major car builders want to tap into.

'Everyone started pulling up in Priuses, nobody wanted to arrive in a Rolls-Royce or Maybach'
Jay Leno, at the Oscars

The current answer is to look towards electricity to power the future car, whether in terms of rechargeable battery power or hybrid systems that combine a traditional engine

The Toyota Auris was launched in HSD (Hybrid Synergy Drive) form, Toyota-speak for a petrol/electric hybrid.

The Lexus RX400h was the world's first production hybrid SUV; this is its successor, the RX450h.

with an electric propulsion system. The first, tentative steps into this brave new world were taken by Toyota in 1997 with the release of the **Prius**. Since then, the Prius has gone from strength to strength and the current generation has some truly startling performance and economy figures. The Prius' petrol engine will produce 98bhp and the electric motor adds a further 36bhp, meaning that when the two are working in unison the car can travel from 0–60 in 10 seconds and reach a top speed of 112mph. Up to speeds of around 30mph the electric motor is quite capable of driving the car on its own, meaning that most inner-city driving will be carried out without the need for the petrol engine. The excellent engine management system means that economy figures of up to 72mpg can be achieved. The 2012 Prius will have the option of a 'Plug-in' system that will further improve the electric motor's performance and allow the Prius to reach electric motor speeds of over 60mph.

As much of the car's city driving requires no fuel and produces zero emissions, not only is it great for the environment, but also for the driver's pocket. The Prius requires no road tax, is exempt from congestion charging and is incredibly cheap to run. Plus, Toyota has a reliability record that, apart from a blip here and there, is second to none. The car comes with all the standard or optional mod cons

With a 3.5-litre petrol V6 backed up by an electric motor, the RX450h offers performance with relative economy.

Even now the Lexus GS450h is the only hybrid executive car; rivals have invested in clean diesel technology instead.

that are expected from a 21st century family car, such as air-conditioning, parking assist, satellite navigation, immobiliser and a decent sound system. The Prius is, however, not without its faults. It is so quiet that pedestrians cannot hear it approaching, creating a safety issue. At prices starting from £21,055 for the basic model, the Prius is not cheap, although considerable savings can be made with running costs during the life of the car.

‘I drive a Lexus hybrid and we have a couple of Priuses in the family’ Al Gore

Another problem is that the Prius cannot be jump started, meaning any cold-morning starting issues will have to be fixed via a call-out service. But these are really only minor issues with what probably represents the future of motoring. The pros far outweigh the cons and Toyota has already released a hybrid version of the **Auris** – its small family car, and more will surely follow.

If there is one car that is the very antithesis of the Prius, it is the SUV. Apart from the size of these vehicles, their fuel consumption is appalling, making the SUV one of the most polluting vehicles on the road. Toyota’s luxury car division, Lexus, had been working on its own hybrid cars throughout the 1990s and it currently offers four hybrids in its UK range; the **luxury compact CT**, the **executive saloon GS**, the **luxury saloon LS** and the **RX**, which is a full hybrid SUV.

The Nissan Leaf is the first production car to be developed from the outset as purely an electric vehicle.

The RX450h is squarely aimed at the luxury SUV market and considering it's a hybrid, it may seem odd that it has a 3.5-litre V6 engine, but this, along with two electric motors (one at the front and one at the back), gives the RX the capabilities of a true 4x4. With the petrol engine engaged at the same time as the electric motor the RX450h can achieve a top speed of 124mph and reach 60mph in approximately 7.5 seconds. Fuel economy sits at around 45mpg, depending on the environment, and the electric motor can power the vehicle by itself up to speeds of 25mph.

Toyota is leading the way in hybrid development and the RX450h shows that SUVs can be both friendly to the environment and appealing to the Kensington housewife. It bodes well for the future of the gas-guzzling SUV and the clear success of the hybrid car has posed the question; can cars be run entirely on electricity?

Ultimately this has to be the aim and there are several cars from around the world that are doing just that. The **Nissan Leaf** was available to fleet companies in Japan and the United States from 2009 and individuals in Hong Kong could buy the Leaf from 2010. The **G-Wiz** has been available in Britain for several years and in the near future many more of these electric cars will flood the market. All across Britain councils are gearing up for the arrival of the fully electric car by installing charge points in car parks and other strategic locations.

'I have two electric cars, but I also have a weak spot because I have flown on private jets' George Clooney

At present, electric cars are hindered by their very low range and they are too expensive to make it worthwhile owning an electric car for local travel and a more traditional car for

driving longer distances. However, the success of the Lexus and Toyota hybrids has ensured that sooner rather than later the electric car will arrive in force and the next revolution in motoring will begin in earnest.

The G-Wiz is perfect for Londoners, thanks to its tiny dimensions and congestion charge-exempt status.

The G-Wiz is great for urban use.

ELECTRIC CARS OF THE 2000S

1. Toyota Prius
2. Toyota Auris
3. Lexus Range (CT, GS, LS & RX)
4. Nissan Leaf
5. G-Wiz

The Mercedes SLS is Mercedes' attempt at a fully-fledged supercar – and it hits the spot perfectly.

Today and Tomorrow

As a new decade gathers pace the car is undergoing some major changes. It began with a raft of austerity measures and as the world tries to recover from one of the worst recessions since the 1920s and 30s car design will once again reflect society's changes.

For the immediate future we can expect more of the same in terms of new cars on the roads of Great Britain. Manufacturers are likely to want to see how the hybrid revolution goes before releasing any further major designs of the petrol-powered car. At the top of the heap, luxury car buyers seem unlikely to take the hybrid route en masse just yet. While Lexus has taken the lead, rivals such as BMW, Mercedes, Audi and Porsche are all set to offer hybrid versions of their mainstream models, while diesel power has started to become the fuel of choice for many buying the largest, most costly cars.

But for the majority of people, new cars may well be a bit of a luxury over the coming years as belts are tightened and people resist the urge to invest in costly outlays in an uncertain

The DS5 marks a return to form for Citroen, a car maker that has spent years in the doldrums thanks to lacklustre design.

Korean car makers such as Hyundai now offer some of the most highly rated cars in the UK. This is its i30 hatch.

world. The global recession and current financial crisis is likely to be mirrored in the cars we see in the future, at least in the short term. Small will continue to be beautiful and the MPV and the SUV will continue to dim the once bright light of the traditional family car. As always, manufacturers are already tempting us with their new models and across the different ranges there are some promising looking cars on the horizon.

The Vauxhall Astra looks superb in three-door GTC form.

The supermini sector will continue to grow and in the next two years many new versions of existing models are due. A new **Renault Twingo** will arrive soon and it comes with a striking new look that will no doubt boost its popularity. This smallest of the Renault range will also feature a sports version that packs a 133bhp 1.6-litre engine, and it looks as though it will give the Clio a worthy challenge for the French company's best small car. Volkswagen will replace the unsuccessful Fox with the imaginatively named **up!**, as its contribution to the supermini market. There will also be new superminis from Kia and Ford, which has announced a new **Fiesta ST**, which squeezes 180bhp from its 1.6-litre Ecoboost engine. Packing that sort of power, the little car can manage 0–60mph in under 7 seconds.

The hugely talented Volkswagen up! is sure to attract keen interest in the city car market.

> 'Everything that can be invented has been invented'
>
> Charles H. Duell, Commissioner, US Patent Office, 1899

In the small family car sector a facelifted model from Hyundai, the **i30**, was in production in 2012. The South Korean manufacturer has been steadily improving over the last few years and the i30 has proved to be a real breakthrough car for Hyundai. There are also planned new models from Audi, Skoda and Ford. Vauxhall released a new **Astra GTC** in 2011. The three-door hatchback has a very appealing, futuristic design and looks like it will be a promising addition to the Astra range, further heaping the pressure on the Focus. In retaliation, Ford will release the **Focus Econetic** in the near future, which claims to deliver fuel economy figures of up to 80mpg, from a petrol engine, which will make the battle between eco-engines and hybrids all the more interesting.

On the hybrid and electric car front, new models from Citroen, Volvo, Audi and Toyota promise to keep the green revolution going. The **Citroen DS5** will utilise a diesel/electric hybrid powertrain, which will further add to the hybrid's cause. Volvo is also working on a diesel/electric hybrid and over the coming years almost every single recognisable car manufacturer will enter the hybrid or electric market.

At the upper end of the sports car sector we can expect to swoon over the **SLS AMG Roadster** from Mercedes-Benz, which will do 0–60 in just 3.7 seconds and is also capable of an electronically limited top speed of 197mph. Aston Martin has announced the release of a new **Virage**, while Audi will update the **R8** and has unveiled a revised **A4**, **A5**, **S4** and **S5**. Then there's the **Audi TT RS** that has a 0–60 time of just over 4 seconds and a convertible TTS that is almost as quick. In 2011, Ferrari unveiled its sensational **458 Italia** and Lamborghini took the wraps off its gorgeous **Aventador**. Not to be outdone, Porsche has unveiled a new **Boxster**, shortly to be followed by fresh editions of the **Cayman**, **911** and **Panamera**.

The original Renault Twingo never made it to the UK; the second generation model is now sold in the UK.

The Mercedes SLS AMG is also available in gull-wing coupé form, aping the classic 300SL 'Gull-wing' of the 1950s.

When we look back to the days of the Austin 1100 it's clear that the car has come a very long way in a very short space of time. Ford's Model T changed the world in 1908, and the Austin 1100 appeared on the scene only 54 years later. The jump between those two models was impressive, as was the jump between the Austin 1100 and the Toyota Prius, which occurred in even less time.

The Ford Fiesta has evolved enormously since 1976, and it's still one of the best superminis on the market.

'I do not believe in electric cars and my company will never make one'

Luca di Montezemolo
(Chairman of Ferrari)

Right across the board, car design has increased by exponential degrees in the last 50 years and who would bet against it doing so in the next 50 years? As more potential markets emerge in industrialising countries there will be cars produced to appeal to those markets

New manufacturers will also appear and the consumer's choice will become more varied. The biggest change will almost certainly be in the hybrid arena. The political shifts in the Middle East will make the reliance on oil ever more undesirable and as green issues continue to be voiced, greater efforts will be made to consign the internal combustion engine to the annals of history. At the beginning of 2012 the car is an essential part of modern life and modern culture, which helps to define who we are. Even though it is certain that the future of the car will be very different to its past, our relationship with the cars we drive will continue to develop and flourish, bringing us all many more years of excitement and joy.

The Lamborghini Aventador supersedes the Murcielago.

Toyota continues to develop the Prius with a plug-in version reaching showrooms in 2012.

Index of Cars

A

B

C

D

F

Photographic credits: All photos © magiccarpics.co.uk except for: 26 (a,b,c), 27 (a,b,c) , 56 (a,b,c), 57 (a,b,c), 94 (a,c), 95 (a,c), 162 (a,c), 218 (a,b,c) © Getty Images; 7, 18 (a,b), 19a, 42, 43, 44, 49, 80, 81, 85b, 86, 94, 130, 131, 132, 135a, 144, 146, 153, 163, 181, 186, 187, 191a, 193a, 194b, 195, 200, 201, 206, 236, 237, 252b © Ford via newspress.co.uk; 11, 15, 47b, 85, 135b, 136, 147, 179, 188, 189, 202, 210, 211a, 250b © Vauxhall via newspress.co.uk; 6, 8, 17a, 24, 37, 60, 173, 174, 193b, 198, 199, 207b, 208, 209, 212, 213, 226, 230, 232, 234 © BMW via newspress.co.uk; 22, 126, 135, 150 © Rover via newspress.co.uk; 35, 168 © Jaguar via newspress.co.uk; 28, 33, 216 © Rolls-Royce via newspress.co.uk; 12, 85a, 87 © MG via newspress.co.uk; 72 © Lotus via newspress.co.uk; 122, 170, 171, 172, 228, 229 © Land Rover via newspress.co.uk; 123 © Jeep via newspress.co.uk; 90, 98, 143, 155, 180, 185, 191b, 203, 238, 251a © Volkswagen via newspress.co.uk; 125, 168, 211, 219, 241, 242, 243, 253b © Toyota via newspress.co.uk; 207, 233 © Audi via newspress.co.uk; 182, 247© G-wiz via newspress.co.uk; 149, 154, 191c, 196, 197 © Peugeot via newspress.co.uk; 139, 176, 177, 192, 239, 251b © Renault via newspress.co.uk; 142, 181 © SEAT via newspress.co.uk; 148, 178, 240, 249 © Citreon via newspress.co.uk; 161, 217b, 244, 245 © Lexus via newspress.co.uk; 157 © Bentley via newspress.co.uk; 166 © McLaren via newspress.co.uk; 175, 217a, 235, 248, 252a © Mercedes via newspress.co.uk; 154 © Volvo via newspress.co.uk; 225, 224, 231 © Porsche via newspress.co.uk; 223 © Aston Martin via newspress.co.uk; 204, 205 © Skoda via newspress.co.uk; 214, 215 © Maybach via newspress.co.uk; 222, 253 © Lamborghini via newspress.co.uk; 221 © Ferrari via newspress.co.uk; 227a, 246 © Nissan via newspress.co.uk; 227b © Honda via newspress.co.uk; 221, 225a © Bugatti via newspress.co.uk; 250a © Hyundai via newspress.co.uk.